Stephan Dorre

Let's try that again

Tales from a Dutch conductor abroad

Ridero

2024

ISBN 978-83-8384-797-9
Created with Ridero smart publishing system

Contents

> *'Music is a labyrinth with no beginning and no end. Full of new paths to discover, where mystery remains eternal.'*
> *Pierre Boulez*

Introduction

> ***'In opera, there is always too much singing.'***
> *Claude Debussy*

The sun is setting, its faded glow turning the sky a delicate purple. Swallows are dancing in the air and there is the gentle murmur of town in the distance. People happily greeting each other, kids playing and the odd crowing rooster, seemingly ever worried that we might not be awake.

I am sitting on the top terrace of our house, looking into the valley, and I feel lucky. After almost three decades of living and working in England, Nick and I packed up our bags and lives to fulfil a long-standing dream of 'being' in Andalusia.

Nearly a year later, we are still overcome with a feeling of amazement and a happiness we thought we had lost. That feeling of being a child on a long summer holiday, life being simple and 'together' with other people. People you know, but also people you don't know.

I moved to London to study orchestral conducting in the mid-1990s, after graduating from the Utrecht Conservatoire in my home country of the Netherlands. Craving a bigger world in general and being in a true international centre of music making, London and the wider UK became my home and base as a musician for all those years.

I always joke that Great Britain is the one country where you can have a successful musical career even if you don't end up having a great musical career. Music is (only just, I must sadly report) still a huge part of everyday life there: a prominent element in school education which feeds a thriving amateur music scene. Most towns will boast an ensemble of some sort, and the bigger cities have several strong non-professional symphony orchestras and opera companies, harmoniously existing side by side with the professional ones. World renowned soloists will gladly perform, and at times big name conductors will be happy to step onto their rostrums.

Staying put after my studies enabled, or maybe even caused, me to live an incredibly busy and satisfying life of conducting, playing and teaching. I still go back regularly for those very things, and inevitably I have started to look back more purposefully at my time and journey on the extraordinary island.

Reminiscing with friends and colleagues about my wonderful teachers, the early years of the opera productions, and the first chapters of conducting my regular orchestras. And through that, starting to realise there is so much more to this than just being able to beat a pulse efficiently. But also watching young musicians study and develop in times that seem a lot harder than they were for us. There is so much less funding available for professional courses, and the financial or even practical support for music in schools is slowly drying up. And we were so fortunate to have had such an incredible bond with our musical elders, a bond that inspired and enabled us so very much.

In the end, Brexit was the main moment we realised that the focus of our musical life would have to lie outside the UK. It seemed crucial to us to be part of Europe, not just musically, but culturally too. It gifts us this ever enriching and refreshing source of exchange, opportunity and inspiration.

Everyone told me that I had to write it all down. And I wanted to, especially after having made a start in the surreal years of Covid lockdowns, when weekly blogs were a wonderful way to stay in touch with the musical family of our orchestras. But I was also beginning to think more and more that my own colourful journey could inspire others, be it professionally or as a means to get a greater insight into what being a musician and being a conductor is all about. And with that, hopefully bringing more enjoyment when seeing and hearing performances.

Reading it back, at times I cannot believe how mad a rollercoaster this journey has been. But definitely one that enabled me as a musician, and I now realise, also as an adept passenger on this overwhelming trip in the grown-up world of music.

Opening night

> *'An opera begins long before the curtain goes up and only ends long after it has gone down. It starts in my imagination, it becomes my life, and stays part of my life long after I have left the opera house.'*
> *Maria Callas*

Nothing could have prepared me for what was about to unfold over the next three hours. In rehearsals, it had become quite clear that steering an opera wasn't as straightforward as just putting together the singers, orchestra and staging. It turned out to be much more of a spectacle than I could ever have imagined.

This was my first production at the helm of one of London's longest established amateur operatic companies. And it was also my first job out of music college. After many months of preparation, opening night was now upon us. The stage and technical rehearsals had admittedly been colourful, but things seemed reasonably in hand.

Arriving at the theatre that evening, I was greeted by a panicky orchestra Leader who took me aside to meet the new bassoon player who was replacing, at rather short notice, the lady who had been rehearsing with us up until that point. The slight problem was that our new recruit was suffering from extreme claustrophobia and had made it abundantly clear that she couldn't possibly play in an orchestra pit. It briefly crossed my mind that this might have been a fact that would have made her decide against taking on this particular engagement, but clearly it had not.

She demanded two square metres of empty space around her or would refuse to take part. In the reality of most orchestra pits, two square metres means a complete brass and percussion section, so this was out of the question. But as she was the only bassoon player available that night, a solution had to be found.

And so, the performance started as planned, with the serene sounds of the prelude, in full darkness, with the curtain down. But now also with a lonely bassoon player in front of it, fully lit and on a golden chair to make it all look less businesslike. What the audience made of this I will never know, but hopefully they saw it as a deep and meaningful touch of stage design, a revelatory vision of the Director, perhaps?

She was not the only last-minute replacement. The original timpanist, who in fairness had only made half a rehearsal himself, had decided it was all too much and sent a deputy as well. My confidence wasn't raised by the new player's comment that she had never really played timpani before. Nor the hastily added assurance that she had always loved playing the triangle in her school brass band. But by now it was too late to worry. *Un ballo in maschera*, a company classic and favourite, was waiting to unfold!

The first scene went well, which was a big relief. But when it came to the opening aria of Amelia, our tragic heroine of Verdi's tale of love, passion and ultimately betrayal (like most of them, it has to be said), we were slightly alarmed that smoke was starting to seep from beneath the closed curtain. When the curtain was raised, it became clear that the dry ice machine, and/or its handlers, had gone into overdrive. Thick layers of fog obscured everything. Nothing (and no one) was visible, and soon the dense clouds also covered the orchestra below in our little musical basement.

I could just about see over the smoke, and detected, like a vague, ghostlike silhouette, Amelia, desperately trying to find her bearings. She was clearly unable to see anything herself, so decided to just start singing, hoping things would look (and sound) up from then on. It took us in our foggy pit by surprise, and meant we had to play catch up for a few exciting moments. But somehow, we managed to reconnect with our lead soprano. Relying on lots of musical and 'stage-spatial' intuition, we got through the aria, be it to a background of loud coughing noises as the smoke had started to get into people's lungs on and off stage.

The curtain came down for the scene change, and a few minutes later I got the little green light telling me to start the orchestral music for the next part. Sadly, however, the curtain didn't actually open, and we soon ran out of 'singer-less' music. I stopped the orchestra, at which point the curtain jittered up, revealing the chorus, half dressed, and looking in a state of shock at being eye-to-eye with the audience.

The curtain rattled down again, and I started to receive frantic instructions from the Director who was 'scream-whispering' from the wings. We had to delay, as our fortune teller Ulrika had gone on strike over her hastily adapted costume.

Both mezzo-sopranos filling this crucial part were pillars of the company, with many, many years of experience and vibratos to match. Probably in an attempt to go against stereotyping, the design of their costumes had turned out a bit, well, 'quirky' to say the least. A pink bodystocking, multi-coloured ribbons decorating their breasts, and that was about it.

Neither diva was happy with this, and I could see their point to be fair, so after some fraught telephone calls more neutral overgarments had duly been arranged. However, these seemed to have mysteriously disappeared now that the actual moment had arrived, and Ulrika was having none of it, boldly refusing to make an entrance. Trying to avoid a disaster, chorus outfits had to be swapped and handed down to her, which was a process that took far longer than hoped. Our star fortune teller had to look the part after all, and the chorus were dressed as unassuming peasants.

Things weren't helped by the fact that she then had to climb up a wobbly plastic tree and sing her opening passages whilst balancing in some sort of 'Tarzanic' hut. Health and safety were not that much of a concern in those days. After about ten minutes, the curtain suddenly opened with Ulrika halfway up the tree, forcing us into unexpected musical action. But she beat us to it and spontaneously started to sing, in a panicky reflex, and 60 bars too soon. More musical catching up followed, a technique we fine-tuned to perfection that week. Just like the 'Not yet please!' arm position I came to firmly rely on. This was not something we were taught at

music college, but totally fundamental in the world of amateur operatics.

We survived the rest of the Act relatively unscathed, if slightly traumatised. At least now there was some time to breathe and regroup. I did allow myself a few sips of white wine. But when I entered the singers' dressing room, I was a bit alarmed to see the rate at which some principals were downing glass after glass of the stuff. Nothing could stop them, I realised, so I just showered them with essential words of praise, as I remembered to do from vocal coaching lessons at college, and rounded everyone up for Act Two.

We scuffled back into our little dark world beneath the stage, and I gave a quick wave to the bassoon player who seemed to be very happy on her golden throne and in her private spotlight.

I then hear mumblings and scrunching sounds, and the first cellist hands me a little crumpled up piece of paper. 'Oh God, not another ******* poem!' the Leader whispers, but just a bit too loudly, making even our on-stage orchestral colleague peer down into the pit with an alarmed look. Fear of heights was not an issue, luckily.

The principal flute player smiles at me, almost naughtily. Her attitude was relentlessly positive, her flute playing ability not inconsiderable, and as we were about to find out, music wasn't her only artistic outlet. Known to spread poetry through Britain's orchestral ranks, this little gem was especially for me, and one that made me blush a bit, I won't lie. She was clearly impressed with my presence, and not just musically. Her choice of words, even if they didn't rhyme at all, left very little to the imagination. I didn't know how to look back at her, and our Leader couldn't stop swearing.

The green light came to the rescue. This unexpected poetic interlude had delayed things, and the Director was manically waving at us. The Act went smoothly, and our confidence picked up. That was until the inevitable Chorus of Conspirators, an essential ingredient in Verdi operas. As there were only six male chorus members, the Director had devised a clever 'rotating walk-ography'. Walking in a circle, before moving off-stage through the back curtains, and then coming back on again, suggesting an endless stream of conspirators... sort of.

In rehearsal, the routine had been close to flawless, but at this crucial moment the mini procession disappeared, only to not reappear again. Where they had gone, no one knew. Afterwards, our ageing but dapper comrades couldn't quite recall what had happened. But when they'd eventually ended up in the dressing room, the decision had been made not to attempt a stage come-back but to enjoy some more wine instead. Alas, the accompaniment for this scene is not one of Verdi's most imaginative orchestral creations, best described as 'plonk-plonk, plonk-plonk'. Four whole minutes of it, as we were still hoping for a glorious return of the gentlemen. Sadly, it was not to be.

Thankfully, without any further incidents, we moved towards the end of the opera. Renato successfully murdered. Amelia suitably distressed. And all of us, singers and orchestra, finishing at roughly the same time, which was a real triumph. Oh, how your musical aim for a performance can change in the course of a few hours!

Just before I went to take a bow, the timpanist thanked me for the opportunity, even though she hadn't played a single note during the whole performance, merely looking shocked every time I had cued her. I shook her hand, took my bow and fled home on the Tube... A different musician, a wiser man, and in need of much wine myself.

London calling

> *'I remember, as a boy, how terrifyingly real the statues of the Saints would seem at mass at seven in the morning, before breakfast. From that I learned to always conduct hungry.'*
> *Leopold Stokowski*

My life was ready for its London chapter.

Alexander Warenberg, who taught me through my final year at the Utrecht Conservatoire, had urged me to shorten my solo diploma studies and make the move to what he called 'a real place' as soon as I could. In his opinion this was essential for my growth, both musically as well as personally, and he was right.

I had been incredibly lucky with the amazing people in my musical life up to that point. Whilst still at secondary school, there was joy, inspiration and friendship from my first serious piano teacher Didi, followed by an essential, if rather dour year of strict, no-nonsense reality from the Director of the Utrecht Conservatoire, Ton Hartsuiker. The biggest compliment he ever gave me was that a particular Bach prelude was 'not bad'. From his mouth, after months of him mainly showing quiet disappointment, this was like fireworks going off. But my time with him got me a place at the Conservatoire. And made me practise. Properly practise.

Alan Weiss became my main teacher in Utrecht, and he turned out to be a huge influence in my life. A phenomenal player with a solid international career, his level of musical instruction was astounding to all of us in his class. Technically and musically, he was very detailed and critical, but it always came from a point of positivity, and a keenness to go on that journey of exploration and development together. He could scream in excitement, use the rudest (but totally appropriate) words and phrases, hug us and shake us. He loved us as young musicians, but also as people, which was a real privilege. Apart from the teaching side, Alan would share the musical world of his own heroes with us, coming from his student days at Julliard in New York.

We would spend weekends at his house in Belgium, pulling all-nighters watching videos of Joseph Hoffman playing Rachmaninoff, Vladimir Horowitz at his total peak, Josef Lhévinne, Vladimir Sofronitsky (a name that I had shamefully not even heard of) and so much more. We would try out new pieces to each other, sight-read (badly) though duets and concertos, and cuddle-up with his better half, Bonzo the chow-chow. Then, when the sun came up, we would walk across the little football pitch opposite his house to the village, where the bakers had bread and croissants fresh from the oven... Much coffee, a train back to Utrecht, and collapse, being richer people.

This shaped us as musicians in a way that you rarely see these days. We were so fortunate that Alan showed such a real interest in us students as human beings, and that we were able to enjoy such wonderful music and life moments at his house. I know we all look back feeling lucky to have escaped the times that were ahead. And I am proud and happy that Alan is still a great friend today, 35 years after our first lesson.

All this stood in stark contrast to the general mood and attitude at the Utrecht Conservatoire. Favouritism, and a total lack of interest in most of the students was everywhere under the management at the time, as well as amongst the teaching staff. We were fortunate that the few islands of good in the sea of institutional sharks were very vocal and supportive, so we got through.

The satisfaction you could feel, especially from the Director and his sidekick Head of Keyboard when slating a student publicly after a performance or exam, was shocking. Yet we lived with it and learned to laugh it off. I remember how my friend felt quite proud when she was told that the only things that were missing from her performance of the three *Klavierstücke* by Schubert were 'dry ice, a white grand piano and candelabra.' She thought this was praise indeed!

Maybe Alan's blanket of positivity was not always the best thing for us though. I remember how he once told me that the idea I had behind a phrase I had totally messed-up in the Chopin *Barcarolle* was 'near genius'. He should probably have told me to practise harder.

Our skins toughened through being on the other side of the judges' table, and that was a good thing mostly. Although I do think that a certain layer of not daring to take myself too seriously as a professional pianist, that little voice, that candelabra, stems from years of their joyous slatings.

For my final solo diploma year, I changed teachers and was very fortunate to be awarded a place in the class of Alexander Warenberg. He was another fantastic pianist, his manner totally different, but equally inspiring. But also known to read a newspaper during some students' lessons, and I still feel honoured that he never did that to me.

Warenberg was strict, had no time for lack of practice, and would happily send us home if we hadn't done enough of it. But he always showed a total respect to us, and it was clear he wanted to make sure we developed the right attitude for the tough career that might be ahead of us.

He was a man of metaphor. Some personal favourites still ring through my head today (and you must try to hear this in a beautiful, almost singing Russian accent): 'Russians travelled by horse, not train!' after my first attempt at Rachmaninoff. 'Have you lost your mind? We are in the Ural Mountains, not the Ardennes!' after my second. But his main, and much-repeated mantra was 'Don't unwrap any presents before you give them.'

When I had finally got to grips with Rachmaninoff's epic Second Piano Sonata, after a year of blood, sweat and tears, and thought I had given it my all, feeling exhausted and with sore fingers, he stood up and gave me a warm pat on the shoulder. 'That was really good', he said, 'but if after the lava stream of the volcanic eruption that is this piece, one little tree pops back up, then sadly you have failed!' That man owned the truth.

We were sitting in the Assistant Director's office at our music college in London. My fellow conducting student and I had only just met, and we were awaiting the arrival of Dr C who was going to enlighten us on the year ahead.

The meeting turned out to be a short one. A brief handshake and an even briefer 'well-wishing ritual' for our success in the college auditions were followed by him telling us, almost with glee, that the college 'didn't offer a conducting course as such.' Having just returned from the Bursar's Office and parted with £5,000 (which, in 1996, was a lot of money), this particular news was not quite what we had hoped to hear.

Being here in London at all was a surprising outcome of my post-Utrecht conducting plans. As a city, London was a huge favourite of mine in which to go and study. But with the college offering only a postgraduate course, I had come to the auditions earlier in the year mainly to see what would be expected of us, and was then planning to take a few undergraduate years in Germany first. The auditions for the London course were a lot earlier than the German ones, so it all fitted in well.

Conducting orchestras was something I had wanted to do passionately for many years. I remember vividly going to a serious orchestral concert for the first time in my life. I was about 10 years old, in the Amsterdam Concertgebouw, hearing Bruch's Violin Concerto played by Raphael Oleg, followed by a Bruckner symphony. I think it was Bruckner 6, but I can't recall that completely. It was serious stuff for my young ears though, I do remember that. That sound of the orchestra, a sound that floated in the air, seemed unreal somehow, but it was mesmerising, and it took me to a magical place. It totally overwhelmed me and made me realise what it was like to feel happy.

The local youth orchestra I ended up playing in, as one of seven flautists, never quite made me reach those same heights of musical ecstasy. The infamous DOJO (Doorns Jeugdorkest) was well-known for performing the same five pieces of music over and over again, all to a dismal standard. Our heroic conductor frequently had to stop us in concerts when things had gone too far down the musical drain. He would look at us, his eyes showing huge disappointment. 'Guys, is it really THAT difficult?', always followed by a big sigh...'Let's go again from letter G.' Even our own parents started to come-up with excuses to stay away.

The highlight was the German guest conductor, Herr S, Maestro of our sister orchestra from Steinheim, stopping the applause after an admittedly rather improvised ending to the *Hall of the Mountain King*. He told the audience that this mess should not be rewarded, before making us re-do the final accelerando and presto section. It was equally chaotic. The audience looked perplexed and a little scared, not knowing if they should put their hands together, possibly giving us a misguided sense of achievement which might hinder our road to musical greatness.

Maestro S saw there was no hope and threw his arms in the air, making our supporters feel they could at least show some appreciation for our lively, be it flawed, efforts. The ovation that followed was of epic proportions.

Over the years the orchestra did improve a lot, even producing a Christmas LP (now a local museum piece, I imagine),

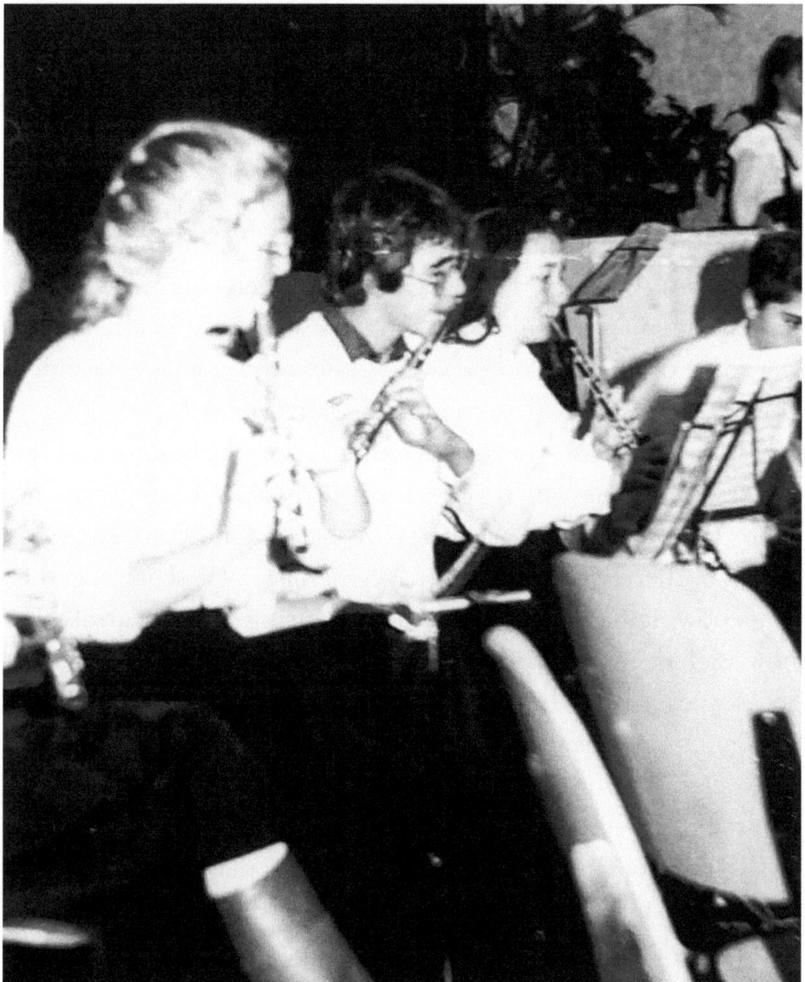

leading to near fistfights over who would play the woodwind solos, but also bringing us some local fame.

It was at this time I developed a real interest in conducting.

In my last year there, and when my piano studies had become seriously geared towards going to music college, I was lucky to be asked, together with a very talented violinist, to be soloist in a movement of Mendelssohn's Concerto for Piano, Violin and Strings. As well as learning that it wasn't a good idea to hastily cut off a rattling button from my performance jacket just before the concert (as it gave me a lively wound which an emergency plaster could only suppress with limited effect, leaving some dramatic blood stains on the keys), I also by accident ended up giving my first conducting performance.

With the orchestra running on a very tight budget and trying to save money, my friend and I had created a performance score by writing out the parts by hand. Our conductor had never bothered to stick the pages of our DIY score together. Somehow, it hadn't been a problem during the rehearsals. But now, a few minutes into the performance, the pages started to escape, leaving him flustered and not quite knowing what was going on. It was never a conscious move, but I found myself instinctively, from the keyboard, cueing in the different sections and actively keeping the speeds together.

It felt so natural and exciting to be playing this as part of a team, rather than just floating in front of the orchestra, and a spark ignited there and then. I knew I wanted to take this conducting thing more seriously. Just imagine being 'in' that floating orchestral sound I remembered from that first Bruch concerto. Being able to create sound worlds and emotional worlds together with the players and share it with other people. I was hooked.

During my piano studies in Utrecht, I was always busy with musical activities outside the college. Playing concerts on two pianos with my former teacher Didi, bringing so much fun and musical enjoyment (if not always total precision and detail) and being lucky to work with singer Hans.

Hans was a well-known baritone in Holland and simply one of the most wonderful human beings in the world. He and his life partner Gert offered friendship and a feeling of belonging to me, as a pianist, but also as a young gay man finding himself. Their generosity was amazing and brought a happiness that has always been an essential part of me since, and which still enables me to face most emotional challenges head on.

Being able to make music with Hans was a complete gift. He made the words and sentences of the poetry guide the musical flow, thinking lines, not notes, and the emotion he could generate in his singing would create shockwaves at times. All of it has shaped how I feel music and perform it. And there was always laughter, incredible laughter.

Nothing was ever more important than life itself, and somehow that brought everything together, music and being alive! And it put the attitude of the music college management (which was the complete opposite) into perspective, making it easier to duck those white grand pianos and candelabras.

Didi had asked me if I would be interested in becoming a conductor of the local string orchestra. It was a group she knew well, had performed with a lot, and who found themselves conductor-less having lost their front man to unexpected (and short-lived, it turned out), composition fame. I said yes, and luckily met with the orchestra's approval. The players were, bar the odd exception, in the more advanced stages of their playing years, but very energetic, and with a huge wealth of experience.

I started from scratch, bought a book on how to beat time and a pile of pocket scores, and at the age of 16, my conducting journey began for real. I always think that my efficiency in conducting orchestras comes from the fact that I was able to start 'on the job'. There was never a 'you should do this' or 'you should look like that.' No aping of learned moves, but only 'what works' – or more often than not, 'what doesn't work.'

The concerts weren't always the finest, but for the development of my skills, both technically, as well as people management-wise, they were worth their musical weight in gold. But even though I felt I was making decent progress, I never thought that my level at this point would get me into the postgraduate conducting course of a leading European music college.

The audition in London had taken place over two days. The first day was an interview, playing the piano and a short conducting test, with the panel singing back Haydn's Symphony No.104, and with us 'air-conducting' the first of Stravinsky's *Dances Concertantes.*

As I had no real formal training in conducting, apart from a few sporadic sessions at college and the experience with my little Utrecht orchestra, I knew only how to prepare as I always did. Not by learning to play a score on the piano or harmonically analysing it, but by learning the music by what it sounded like through listening to different recordings, knowing the instrumental cues, and having a clear idea of what the musical language should bring across. The same as I would do learning my piano parts when working with singer Hans or playing chamber music in a larger group.

I noticed the panel was whispering in an approving tone after my conducting, and the Chair even said it was the first time they had managed to sing the Haydn together that day, and in tune. At that point I didn't know whether to take it as praise or sarcasm, my Utrecht years having taught me never to expect a proper compliment.

Next up was a hilariously difficult theory test, which literally made the guy next to me fall off his chair (although afterwards, we felt his seat had probably been sabotaged by one of the other candidates). Guessing intervals that stretched more than two octaves, trying to play a score with five different transposing instruments, and writing down an excerpt from a rather avant-garde string quintet. It would make anyone jump to the floor and got us to talk and laugh and decide to de-stress by visiting a Redon exhibition at the Royal Academy. We were both convinced that we wouldn't get through to the second round of auditions, so making the most of this incredible city, centre of all the arts, centre of all people and cultures, was a no-brainer. This is what Warenberg had wanted for me. And here I was, even if just for a few days. So, we lapped it up.

Redon's paintings proved so addictive that we lost track of time and had to rush back to check the list pinned on the college wall (very Lutheran), with the names of the candidates who had made it through to the second day and the round of conducting the college symphony orchestra. And there was mine, one of only six. I was shocked.

Suddenly plans to go and see *The Valkyrie* at English National Opera, had to go out the window and be replaced with more score study, and trying to act the part the next day. (ENO was a new one for me, thoroughly stuck in my Dutch musical upbringing which taught us that translated operas were blasphemy).

The following morning, I watched the candidate before me tackle the Haydn. He was a very experienced-looking conductor, who was bombarding the orchestra with his wisdoms on string technique, woodwind articulation, and detailed knowledge of what the composer was going through at the time they composed the piece. I felt quite intimidated, as clearly there was no hope, just the opportunity for a great experience to take with me.

My Haydn went well. I was impressed by how the players followed my dynamic suggestions, without me actually telling them anything, and the speeds were all as I had hoped. But there was little reason to stop and rehearse, apart from asking for the staccato notes to be a bit shorter. Stravinsky proved trickier, as the orchestra seemed to revert to a slower speed than I had in my mind and that I was trying to indicate. In this speed, things got messy and rhythmically inaccurate.

The Chair of the panel came up to me and suggested I should try to beat out the quavers and take up the slower speed. Ugh, not good, a slight feeling of failure – but hey, I might as well try! I managed to do it mostly, being totally unprepared. But at times the irregular bars caught me out, as I was not now beating the longer or shorter beat units but all the quavers individually. We got there in the end, but it was not what I had hoped for, and I walked away a bit deflated.

Whilst I was having a quick coffee in the college foyer before taking the Tube to my hotel, the guest conductor on the panel came up to me and took the time to say how impressed he was with how I had coped with the request to change the way I was beating the Stravinsky. He said that the orchestra were not familiar with that piece and had rehearsed it much slower than the metronome marking, and in quavers, as they didn't expect that someone would take it in tempo, especially not by beating the combined quaver beat units. Pat on the shoulder, and a quick wink.

The little corner where my coffee was still sitting had now been taken over by some players from the orchestra, who greeted me enthusiastically. In their opinion, I was the only candidate that day who had given them an actual beat to play off, and therefore there had been no need to stop all the time. My Stravinsky attempt was by far the least disastrous one apparently, and even in the pre-audition rehearsal with Dr C, it had been carnage.

'Technique' they called it, which was that word that was both scary and alien to me. What technique should I have? What should I look like when beating time? What does it even mean? But they liked it and said they'd be surprised if they didn't see me after the summer. I thought this was kind but at the same time didn't believe it at all.

I had a lovely afternoon ahead, more galleries and a meal in China Town with a friend of a friend. Except this friend of a friend spent the whole meal telling me that the Guildhall was so prestigious, that I would most likely not get in, and that I shouldn't feel ashamed about it. He was probably trying to be supportive, but his tactics were failing miserably. My flight home was the following morning, giving me time to prepare for a German language exam, and then the Hamburg and maybe Vienna auditions to follow in the spring.

Sitting on the steps of the National Gallery and looking at Trafalgar Square, alive with tourists and the water from its fountains glisteningly golden in the sunshine, I couldn't help but hope that the players were right. I had totally fallen in love with London.

Six weeks later, and in the middle of preparing for my final piano recital and the Hamburg application, the letter came. I was at my parents' home, speaking on the phone with my old flute teacher about a youth orchestra concert, when my Mum put it in front of me, unopened. My old flute teacher was lovely, but also someone who wouldn't stop talking once on a roll. And her roll was properly on now, meaning I couldn't get a single word in for 15 minutes, which felt like an hour, whilst my heart rate was going up and up. In the end I just opened the letter and saw the sentence inviting me to join the course staring back at me. I rudely cut her off mid-sentence. 'I got into the London music college!!! I'll phone you back!' and abruptly put the phone down on her. It was a no-brainer for me. I cancelled the Germany plans and geared my life towards the city of my dreams.

So, here I now was, £5,000 poorer and with no course as such, but at the start of this new life chapter.

Just finding a place to live in London had turned out to be an epic undertaking. I was hoping to move into a flat with the daughter of amazing friends from Wiltshire. We shared Dutch family history, and personal life had been quite a journey for all of us these last few years. It created a family bond that is as strong today as it was then.

We spent weeks and weeks getting up early, buying the *Loot*, that magical daily newspaper with all those adverts for rooms and flats (and anything else you could wish for: husbands and wives, plumbers and pet rabbits...), phoning up as quickly as we could, still in pyjamas, before racing to town to view the potential properties. It all took a lot longer than we'd hoped, and our plan to share a flat sadly had to be abandoned before it had become a reality. So, I ended up commuting from the Wiltshire family home for the first few weeks of the course, before finally finding a room on my own in central London.

Located in very gay-friendly Earl's Court, the entrance to my building was next door to the local *Clonezone*. A shop for anything you could think of, and could never think of, in the field of sexual enjoyment. The window displays were without fail spectacular, mind-boggling and at times tear-inducing. On their first visit, when delivering some much-needed Dutch supplies, my dear parents parked up just in front of it, mistaking the shop door for mine. Seeing their faces when they finally got upstairs was a moment I will never forget.

My room was in a large apartment, part of a 1930s block. It was all run by a German lady, named after an infamous Greek mythological character of dubious reputation. And if 'nomen est omen' was ever appropriate, it was here.

Until this point, I had always had this naïve feeling that people were basically okay, and if you behaved and treated everyone reasonably well, you would get the same back. But this utopian vision was shattered in theatrical manner by the German-Greek flatmate.

Short, orange dyed hair, sharp facial features and a penetrating voice, her accent being almost caricature, she was initially over-friendly. Like we were destined to be best buddies forever, here in this apartment. We could share everything: meals, baths, evenings in front of the television... it seemed she had hoped it would be like a commune. 'Please keep your door open, I always do!', I remember her suggesting.

Her love life was colourful, and more significantly for us, very, very loud. Clearly, pain was something fabulous in her experience. But the noisy expression of it was keeping us awake night after night – although I was amused that it normally unfolded to the music of *Carmen* (the *Toreador* song was a favourite): a nice touch, and ironically quite appropriate.

She studied experimental art and used every part of the flat to try out new, and quite extreme, media. Breaking just about anything that got in her way in the process, she was keen to point the finger of blame at the other flatmates without any shame. When I suggested she should just be honest and pay for the damage, she pinned a drawing of a child's head to my door with a big kitchen knife. It could have been up for a Turner Prize, but it didn't bode well for the time ahead.

From that moment on, I was clearly on her 'get-rid-of' list, culminating in her lying about rent arrears and telling me I had a week to leave. I tried to speak to the official landlord, but before I could get through, and just returning from a weekend with my friends, I found all my belongings on the street with a note saying she wouldn't charge me for the last week's rent so that I could pay for a hotel. And in her eyes, that was a very generous move. In a state of disbelief, I was too stunned to think properly and decided to phone my grandmother from the phone box just opposite the *Clonezone.*

My Oma was a total hero in my life. Living through the Second World War in Amsterdam with a little baby taught her always to be positive and to develop the art of looking at situations from a distance. Step away and make it into a film almost. She had been a rock through tricky times before I came to London and proved to be that rock again. She told me to picture the scene and explain it to her, like I was describing a theatrical set:

> *Well, this is central London. I am looking at a shop window filled with colourful sex toys, and mannequins with masks and harnesses. My chair is standing in front of the door of it, next to suitcases with my clothes and books. And my childhood teddy, Skolly, seems to smile at me from the top of the pile...*

Whilst I was describing all this to her, the ridiculousness of it struck me, and I burst out laughing. She asked me if I was okay, and if I had a place to go, which I had, as my amazing friend could

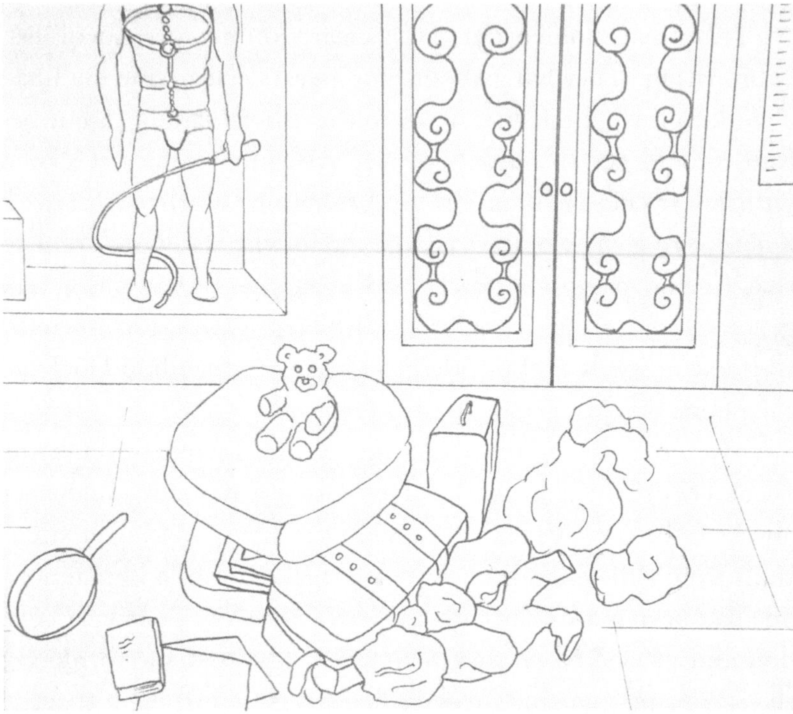

take my things and my hero Nick was happy for me to stay with him in his room in Islington... a true test of a one-month-old relationship (which was effortlessly passed, it must be reported).

She ordered me to write it down as a possible operatic plot twist, have some G&Ts on her with Nick, and laugh it off. No one was dying, and amazing people were there to help. And lucky new developments meant that I could move in with my friend in lovely Putney Bridge soon after, making our original plans come true in the end, bringing a calm home base that had been missing until then.

A life lesson was learned, 'nomen est omen'! Thank you, Oma, always.

My fellow postgraduate student at the Guildhall came from the mainstream British music education circuit. He had studied at one of the top UK universities, where the conducting teacher was well known, if slightly infamous for his perceived lack of musical taste. And my fellow student's beat was a fabulous one, it must be said, something our theory teacher and I agreed upon. But we also agreed that conducting an orchestra successfully was not just about that, as was going to become very clear over the course of the next nine months.

Mr Grump, as he soon became known, didn't seem to take much notice of me, barely spoke before or after the lessons, and he was not very present at college on a day-to-day basis. During the first week, and at a few hastily organised Freshers' events, I had made contact with a nice double bass player with conducting aspirations, and I spent a lot of time with him and his friends in those early months.

It had become clear that we needed to create our own course in a way, around a few weekly theory lessons and two orchestral masterclasses with the guest conductor mentioned above. As my double bass friend was 'in' with a lot of the string players, it seemed a natural step to plan a string orchestra concert together, with him conducting the Tchaikovsky *Serenade* and me conducting Grieg's *Holberg* Suite. This was a good goal for the first term, and a nice way to get to know more students.

The theory lessons were based mainly around score reading and playing, as well as memorising pieces. A lot of harmonic analysis, the very thing that was such a challenge for me, and very dry matter. Our teacher was a lovely man who seemed a little disappointed and bored by these subjects himself. But he had learned to accept that this is what conducting tuition meant in an institution that didn't really cater for student conductors when it came to practical experience. You could feel a sense of melancholy when he talked about his own times as a conductor, and the work he had done with a South American youth orchestra which was in the early stages of its development back then, but which is now a huge force in the international music world.

He was an excellent teacher, and I remember being surprised that after two particularly analytical hours that were utterly sleep-inducing and which made me question the meaning of life itself, I could play the first movement of Dvořák's Seventh Symphony from memory, viola and French horn lines included. And give a full harmony report if I had been asked for one (something, I have to add, that has never happened in 35 years of conducting orchestras and ensembles). But I still use his method for quick score memorising when pushed for time.

Our course urgently needed creating, so I decided to advertise my piano playing skills and my experience working with singers and instrumentalists to the teachers at the college, who were very keen to take me up on it.

One of the main vocal professors was a formidable mezzo-soprano of respectable fame who had a wealth of technical knowledge as well as stage experience. Her limited English meant that she was flawless in conveying this knowledge in a very instinctive way, by vocally demonstrating from a vast repertoire of 'how not to sound' noises that were frightening, yet totally effective. I heard every singer that she taught transform in her lessons and sing with a warm yet clear sound. I even think I would have had brief moments of Jessye Norman-like vocal splendour if I had undergone the Diva's treatment.

She was also a master of operatic characterisation, and her demonstration of the type of Italian housemaid needed for Mozart's character, Despina, was a performance worth paying good money for and one I often go back to (always paying tribute to the original source, of course).

'Darling', in a glorious Italian accent, like a Roman fountain or a great chianti, 'Despina would not shyly apologise for the food if you would not eat it!! No, no, no! She would come over, show disbelief, firmly put her hand on the table and say, 'why don't you eat this, you stupid idiot, this is the most amazing chicken in the world!!'' She would then spend several minutes 'being' in the Despina character to ram her point home.

She had endless patience, trying again and again until the desired sound and emotion were reached. Her famous catchphrase of last resort was, again in her radiant Italian accent, 'Darling, you must sing from your pussy!' She would tell this to males as well as females. The first time anyone heard this, it always mildly shocked rather than inspired. But soon everyone knew what she meant. And she was totally right of course, we always must! What is the point otherwise?

She was impressed with my sight-reading skills and ability to follow most spontaneous musical escapades, yet also encourage the singers musically. Years of working with singer Hans came in handy there. I gained a busy sideline playing for her lessons and accompanying student concerts.

Perhaps the greatest perk of the course was that the college was in the same building as one of the main London concert halls. Having a strong connection with the resident orchestra, the college was able to offer us passes for all their rehearsals: an incredible 'tool' in the development of any musical skills, but particularly for conducting.

What a difference compared to my homeland, where top professional musical life was so removed from the world of the music student! I remember phoning up the Concertgebouw Orchestra when Georg Solti came to guest conduct with them, asking if it was possible for students to sit in on a rehearsal, or part of it. Without even taking time to think this over, there was a resounding 'No. This is not something we facilitate.' And that was not the only example. A few regional orchestras showed a refreshing difference, but to see the absolute great conductors at work was nigh-on impossible. This was probably not helped by commercial schemes which raised funds by making people pay a lot of money for watching a planned, open rehearsal. Not good when you are a poor student.

Being able to watch amazing maestros rehearse a programme from scratch was a privilege, and eye-opening for us. Well, for me mainly, as Mr Grump had all but disappeared. Colin Davis, Andre Previn, Rafael Frübeck de Burgos, and many more. And all totally different in their approach and sound. What these particular three had in common was that they didn't speak much. No constant stopping and explaining, but letting the music find its flow by just being there with their body language, personality and musical aura. They could give a few simple and quick words of desired character, and the sound would suddenly take shape.

It made me realise that every conductor, every person even, comes with their own sound. It is the most mysterious thing. Put someone in front of an orchestra, let them not say a word, or even move, and their sound will still emerge. Mostly so with Frübeck de Burgos, who in two hours of just being him made the orchestra produce a rich and full sound that was not always their trademark. Their performance that weekend of De Falla's *Nights in the Gardens of Spain*, with the unsurpassable Alicia de Larrocha, was overwhelming and intoxicating. It was a moment when I realised how important this piece was for the performers, and how crucial it was for them to communicate it to us, sharing this amazing gift the composer had given the world.

During a break in rehearsals when I was watching Previn conduct Ravel's *Daphnis and Chloë* (again, one or two brief but crucially judged instructions made the music and the musicians soar), I found the courage to go up to him and ask for his advice to young conductors like me. He took a lot of time to chat and share his own experiences, being very generous and seemingly down to earth. For him, it was all about getting out there and doing it. Find players, set up orchestras if needed, or try to find a position with a 'community orchestra' as he called it.

This filled me with optimism, as that was all I had known until that point, and what the college was, be it unintentionally, offering. Maybe there was 'no course as such', but certainly a wealth of talented young musicians, knowledgeable teachers and performance facilities. And the students at college were very up for taking part in the orchestral or ensemble projects we would organise.

In the UK, being able to sight-read to perfection, and knowing masses of orchestral repertoire, is a crucial element of being a professional orchestral musician. The rehearsals available to the orchestras there are famously few, and there is simply no time to get to know the notes in the short time available. This meant that everyone at college was keen to play as much repertoire as possible and get the major works under their musical belts.

The actual 'making this happen' was not always made easy by the music college management, however. There was one teacher in particular who somehow seemed to feel threatened by these activities and tried to sabotage them wherever he could. Telling his students he could have been a famous concert pianist, a Horowitz, if he had chosen that path, this was a man with a huge ego and beard to match, but with considerably less playing ability to back up his statement. Huffing and puffing, sweating and grunting, he would scramble his way through repertoire, often barely recognisable, whilst talking about the music's virtues at the same time. And on one occasion famously slamming through the piano stool and crashing onto the floor. (They clearly had to sort out their stools and chairs in this place, although there was probably no chance of survival on this occasion). But he was a man with power in the college.

Booked rehearsal rooms could suddenly no longer be available, at times leaving a chamber orchestra stranded and a rehearsal drowned. Concert dates were unexpectedly vetoed due to management meetings suddenly being re-arranged, or keys for the relevant rooms mysteriously disappearing. Drawing from my years of 'white grand piano' comments, having to stand up for myself at the Utrecht Conservatoire, and just my Dutch directness (which is too often like garlic to a vampire in England), I frequently found myself waiting outside the Assistant Director's office to complain. And just as frequently, I was not alone.

A lovely Scandinavian postgraduate violin student was clearly going through similar patterns and emotions. She had also just parted with £5,000 and was urgently wondering where the orchestral playing element was for her 'orchestral' course. We sat on the large white faux leather sofa in the waiting room, exchanging our experiences, before the Assistant Director would call one of us in, with a look of dread, pissed-off-ness and worry, all combined. 'Oh no, not more garlic...'

Every time, the routine unfolded in a similar way. Apologies, and always hoping that in future, things would be made easier. A wry smile and a handshake, then closing the door before we could say thank you. It turned out things very much stayed as they were, that is until my very last concert there. But I had made a new friend who was keen to play for my projects, and we got a few nice concerts and repertoire evenings off the ground, sneaking around the movements of 'could-have-been Horowitz'. I also accompanied her in her lessons, giving me a wealth of knowledge about repertoire, bowing technique and variety of violin sounds and how to achieve them. Her teacher was not seen as the 'main man' in college, but I thought he was excellent and very inspiring, drawing from his years of playing at the highest level with the London Symphony Orchestra.

'Elk nadeel heb ze voordeel' ('every disadvantage has an advantage'), the Dutch football player Johan Cruijff once famously said in that wonderful Amsterdam twang. (Or was it his Rotterdam counterpart Willem van Hanegem?) And it shows to be true, time and time again.

There were two masterclasses that year where we'd be able to conduct the college junior symphony orchestra, under the watchful eyes of the guest conductor and our own teacher. The guest conductor, who had also been part of the audition panel, was a musician of huge experience. First as an orchestral percussionist (when he had been affectionately nicknamed 'Rascal' by Bernard Haitink), then a conductor of youth orchestras, and now starting to build a career internationally. He was a jolly, energetic man of quirky bow ties and slick manner.

The first thing he told us was never to call any player in an orchestra 'Mr-' or 'Mrs Clarinet' as he had done whilst debuting with one of the American orchestras and was promptly never asked back. We joked that it might have been the bow ties instead, which he ignored.

On the programme for this first class was Dvořák's Seventh Symphony. It is a work of huge emotion and lyricism, combined as always with his dance-like happiness, something Dvořák just can't seem to avoid, almost like an apology for the drama. But also, a piece in which there are big decisions to be made: to beat half bars or crotchet beats, full bars, where to take time, where not to take time, and which general speeds to choose. Our teaching maestro didn't go into these aspects much, but focused on grand gesture conducting tips, like a one-man show almost. And these were very useful, often contradicting what our slightly obscure second subject teacher back in Utrecht had tried to convince us of.

Clarity, clarity, clarity, showing the beat and part of the bar for everyone to see. Realising that a huge percentage of the string players are sitting to the sides of the conductor, not being able to distinguish how far to the left or right the click point is happening. 'Upbeat up: crucial. Downbeat down!!! Dorré, stop flapping!' It seems obvious, but you'll be amazed how many conductors' downbeats go up. Very famous ones too! It was a flood wave of his conducting wisdom, and it took me a long time to take it all in. Years later something would suddenly come back to me, and it was always a tool for being more efficient.

But the best thing about the class was our theory teacher, who suddenly came to life with the dust of harmonic analysis blown off. He positioned himself behind the orchestra and took in our every move, instructing us in very clear and perfectly judged words and gestures as we were conducting. Like Previn, or Frübeck de Burgos, just what needed saying or showing: nothing more, nothing less.

And for me it suddenly clicked. Seeing him first imitate my own movements, and then bit by bit almost moulding these into calmer, more focussed and much less jumpy brushstroke-like gestures. The 'flapping' was eliminated there and then. And to my amazement, the sound I had in my ear was also suddenly coming back from the orchestra.

No need to subdivide the final statement, just widening the half bar beat to show the broadening of the tempo. Breathing it with everyone, enabling that majestic last note to be long enough to send the sounds, and the towering masterpiece itself, into the sky and beyond. Without asking, somehow the players created this just from my movements, as transformed by this amazing teacher. It was a huge moment and gave me a massive boost.

There were a couple of official college concerts that we were allowed to conduct. The first was the annual composition competition finals, offering us repertoire ranging from the tentatively 'maybe one day' to the downright ridiculous. There were time signatures that took ages to figure out and musical instructions that made you scratch your head and try to comprehend what on earth the composer might have been after. And which would make the players think of taking out extra insurance for their instruments.

Most of the titles were fantastical and colourful. Although I still feel that naming your piece 'Why Not?' was too much of an open goal to a jury that was keen to bask in superiority and criticising glory. The violin concerto in question was actually a nice piece. But alas, the inevitable opportunity for a one-word judgment proved more appealing to the adjudicating royalty that night. Shame, we all liked it.

The second concert was a wonderful opportunity for us, conducting the college chamber orchestra in the imposing Great Hall of the Bishopsgate Institute in the City of London.

By now, it was early spring, and I had created a good bond with a lot of fellow students. I was flattered to be asked to look after the *Pulcinella* Suite by Stravinsky, whilst my colleague, who had been seen at the college less and less (and who seemed more and more grumpy, doing his new name justice), would conduct the first half, being Mozart's famous Fourth Horn Concerto. Amazing music, with the added responsibility of accompanying to the soloist's wishes. Or so you'd think.

Pulcinella was a dream come true, and the players were fantastic. Totally committed and professional, they made life very easy. The rehearsals went smoothly, and it all sounded just as I had hoped for. Our theory teacher suggested I could conduct without a baton for this one, to see if it would make me find my own body language more, as opposed to moving a stick from left to right and up and down. It was a very worthwhile experiment.

In the end for me, though, using a baton is preferable. It is clearer for the players, and in a way clearer for me. But working without one for several projects made me completely change the way I hold the baton, bringing more character to the beat whilst still maintaining that proper 'inner pulse' which seems to bring calm and a clear understanding to all of us involved.

I did envy Mr Grump's truly beautiful beat. It had a clean click, but also this elegant wave-like flow, it was just great to watch. But this concert showed that it becomes pointless when the tide turns against you.

In rehearsal it had become clear that he had a different idea of the role of the conductor when it came to solo concertos. Not only did he insist on dictating the speed (something the feisty, and very talented horn player was not happy about), but he also changed the phrasings and dynamic additions she had brought to the solo part. In disbelief, our teacher and I watched the rehearsal turn from a musical disagreement into a much more personal fight, with raised voices and increasingly inappropriate word choices. The orchestral players were embarrassed, but clearly supported the soloist.

Our teacher went over and called Mr Grump aside, calming him down, and suggesting it would be great for him, and everyone, to follow the soloist. And possibly discuss any musical ideas afterwards, and in private.

After a short, imposed tea break (we are in England, after all, where tea cures most issues), things seemed to improve. That was until it came to the final *Rondo*, and the slight accent-like emphasis the soloist put on the last note of her opening main statement. It was done with style and panache, and an open invitation to the orchestra to fly with it. Did Mozart write it? No. Was it totally in the spirit of Mozart and the concerto itself? Absolutely!

But it also broke the thin veneer of cooperation from Mr Grump. A cup of tea can only suppress so much. He stopped and made it clear to everyone that he wasn't going to be part of this performance if she insisted on keeping the accented note in. His tone and aggressive manner clearly shook the soloist, who at that moment felt she had no choice but to agree to take the accent out. Maestro Grump was now feeling in charge, and with that, the rehearsal ended. And we all needed a lot more tea.

The day of the concert came, with only a short warm-up rehearsal possible. Just quick starts and stops, and we were on. I was backstage with our teacher, watching the first half.

Mr Grump and the soloist were not really speaking beforehand and came onto the stage quite a distance apart from each other. The first two movements went well, showing what a bright young star the horn player was, and the orchestra seemed to be following the leader more than conductor Grump. Teacher and I, almost ringside, looked at each other and had to admit that his beat really was fabulous.

But now came the last movement, and the end of that first phrase. As it was coming to that last note, the soloist turned to Mr Grump, stared him straight in the eye, and planted an accent so massive on there that it would not have been misplaced in *The Rite of Spring*. Not only that, but the orchestra did exactly the same! It clearly marked a huge show of support for her and was possibly even pre-planned. Behind the stage door, we had to work hard not to burst out laughing. Our heroic horn player continued like nothing had happened, and Mr Grump seemed too rattled to be able to do anything but get through it and let the leader effectively take over. The ends of phrases that followed were beautifully judged by soloist and orchestra alike, and the concerto reached its conclusion without any more excessive bumps.

During the applause, there were massive hugs from leader to soloist, before she walked off, totally ignoring the sheepish-looking Mr Grump, and gratefully basking in the glory she utterly deserved.

Pulcinella was a joy, and another important moment of conducting development for me that year. In the months that followed, we only saw my colleague one more time at college.

London in the mid- to late nineties was a city of optimism and expanding horizons. Under New Labour the UK started to open up to Europe, and with that came a wider exchange of cultures which enriched life in all respects. And it brought out the best of the UK itself. Public services started to improve, and the last shreds of political anti-gay sentiments were broken down bit by bit. I had been shocked by how recently firmly established homophobic laws were being justified and accepted by certain political parties that happened to be in power. But now the UK seemed to be waking up, and it made for the best time to be there.

I met amazing people, one of them still my better half as I write this, and indulged in a total overload of music, visual art and food. Looking back, it was possibly even a bit too much at that point in my life, meaning that complete musical focus was not always there. I could, and should, have learned scores in more detail, and spent more time finding auditions. But I also had to catch up on life somehow and be totally me. Free from other people's perceptions as put on me by the Utrecht Conservatoire, and by myself too. The timing was not so ideal, having just one postgraduate year at the college, but the whole process was essential. And I was so fortunate to have my Wiltshire-based home away from Holland, being able to go any time to regroup and to reconnect with my roots.

Venues like the Royal Festival Hall meant that we could go and see the greatest orchestras in the world for very little money. Maybe they were tiny in the distance and a bit quiet, with us sitting in the back seats, but the magic was no less for it. The Vienna Philharmonic dazzled and frankly showed off with Stravinsky's *Firebird* and Strauss' *Ein Heldenleben* in one programme. Under Lorin Maazel, who was an astounding Director, the musical layers and colours were just unreal. Then Barenboim's Bruckner 9, which was colossal and like a cathedral. And that sound!! You could always get a student ticket and we watched a huge number.

Our own Concertgebouw Orchestra, the Chicago Symphony, the Berlin Philharmonic, it was truly incredible, and we could afford to go! What a difference from the main hall in Amsterdam, beautiful as it was, where the ticket prices were so expensive that there was no way we could see the true greats on a regular basis.

But possibly the biggest discovery for me was opera. Two main companies in one city meant that we were spoilt for choice, and at times found it hard to choose what to go and see. And again, there were affordable tickets available. Fewer maybe for the Royal Opera House, but if you were patient, you could get a ticket even if it meant standing in a queue for a few hours. This was the time of Bernard Haitink's musical leadership, and the orchestra had never sounded better. From Mozart to Wagner, the performances were top-notch, and you could feel that the singers and players wanted to give their best to him, and he to them. Lucky us.

The biggest change for me though came when going to see the ENO. Student tickets were always available, and we saw many operas there.

ENO performs in English, something that in Holland had seemed totally unacceptable. 'The vowels don't fit the music; the music doesn't fit the consonants' – these were the things we were taught and started to believe. Until, that is, my first Coliseum experience: Puccini's *Tritico*. As it cost only a fiver, I had come to terms with the fact that I would probably hate the language situation but would still enjoy hearing all three short operas as intended.

To my amazement, I found myself totally immersed, as I could follow every word directly from the singers' mouths. The story suddenly came first for me, and the music was there to heighten the experience of it. It seemed to bring the best from the actor-singers as well, now more like singing actors, and drawing us all in. There were still surtitles for the moments when orchestral outbursts matched the vocal powers (outbursts which were musically needed and inescapable at times), so we could follow everything. I didn't feel like I was watching a very long concert with people in costumes anymore: I was in the drama.

The ENO also stood out at that time for its riveting productions. Timeless ones by people like Jonathan Miller, mixed with spectacular and effectively updated ones by new and upcoming directors. Of course, there were a few incomprehensible stagings, but they seemed rare.

I still dream sometimes of David Alden's colourful and at times totally insane version of Berlioz's *Damnation of Faust*. It has never left me. From the very first moment, magic happened not only on stage, but also in the audience and on the side balconies, moving us from grey and dark scenes of anarchy and personal emptiness to a world of show, brightness and ultimately insanity.

This amazingly huge fish, sticking out of a bathtub in the mental asylum. Hallucinogenic characters from history coming out of a wardrobe in the often-cut ballet scene. Marilyn Monroe, Fred Astaire, Patsy from *Absolutely Fabulous*...

Willard White, the great American bass baritone, gave us the sexiest devil you could hope for. His main aria sung in a glittery tail suit, with cane and top hat, in the spotlight in front of the curtain. The impact was massive.

On one of the evenings I went to see it (as this was addictive stuff), a candle refused to go out and started rolling, still burning, towards the curtain at the sides. You could see the singers on stage watching nervously, not quite knowing what to do. As if it was part of the staging, and totally in character, White's Mephistopheles swaggered towards the candle, continuing to seduce the ladies and gentlemen in that scene in the process. On a suitable top note, he stamped out the candle in one sweeping gesture. David Alden could not have choreographed it better. On and off stage, we were all totally in awe. Move over Marguerite!

In college, my piano-playing ability also propelled me more and more towards operatic territory.

I had taken specialist lessons in repetiteur skills, learning piano reductions and training myself to be able to 'sing in' a vocal part, as well as play and keep an eye and ear out for what was happening musically. It was a total nightmare at the start, with hilarious sounding results. But bit by bit I was able to hold a particular line, ranging from bass to soprano, all sounding equally horrendous but vaguely recognisable, to present something the other singers could 'sing off'. Increasingly, I got asked to play for rehearsals and lessons, or individual coaching sessions. This last activity was new to me. With my non-operatic background, I innocently thought that a coaching session was like a rehearsal, with me playing and then rehearsing the music to the singer's wishes.

My first attempt, which was with a Scandinavian soprano who was working on an aria from Mozart's *Cosi Fan Tutte*, showed my inexperience. After she had finished the aria, I looked at her expectantly and she looked back at me, followed by an uncomfortable silence. Her look then became quite panicked, and I could feel tension kicking in. I asked her what she wanted to work on. She seemed taken aback and stayed quiet. I suggested we could maybe look at the speed of the aria and see what she would like to do with it. 'But you tell ME that!' she said, still looking slightly spooked and defensive.

I hadn't anticipated that this was the process, but hey. So, I started to chat about the words and emotion and what she wanted to come across from the aria. I said that I thought she sounded great and....boom, there and then her panic disappeared, and with a sigh of relief she said, 'Oh thank you, it normally sounds better at home.' I said I'd find that hard to believe, and that I loved her warm sound and real emotion towards the end of the aria. She sat down, as if to recover from the awkwardness of the last 10 minutes, then finally smiled and asked, 'So, what do you want me to do with the aria?'

It started to dawn on me that I was not the pianist here to rehearse with her. First, I must make it very clear that she was fabulous and wonderful, which she was, and then tell her how to sing it. And never present anything as less than a triumph, just explore how this triumphant-ness could be heightened even more.

The world of opera really was very different to what I knew from working on *Lieder* with singer Hans and others back in Holland. And it is fair to say that this hard-earned knowledge carried me through a decade of amateur opera in London, and professional work beyond that.

It was now nearly summer, and the end of the academic year started to come in sight. I was passionately getting through what we now refer to as our 'French arthouse movie period' in my still growing relationship with my better half, easily matching most films and TV series in full-on emotional drama. But there was so much more!

Neighbours' electric blankets catching fire, with us ending up in the street in the middle of the night. We returned there an hour or so later, just when the smouldering mattress, which had been placed against the wooden porch, caused both to light back up in cosy harmony. This being London though, it seemed the only way to meet your neighbours, and they turned out to be delightful company.

Idyllic boat trips from Putney bridge to Kew Gardens in the spring and enjoying tea on the tombstones, a popular picnic spot clearly, at the little church cemetery. It was another first for me.

Eating the best Chinese and Thai and Indian and Lebanese meals. And most rewarding of all maybe, enjoying the famous black London cabs! They were always just a finger click away. It was just incredible to a Dutch person, and too tempting, especially in those French movie months. There were many desperate midnight taxi journeys to iconic train stations: it was all very Truffaut. But it also caused my scholarship to run out spectacularly several months early. I still owe my parents a Greek villa with pool once monetary fortune finally hits, as a way to say thank you for bailing me out.

We had our second and last masterclass of the year with the guest conductor, but sadly his mind seemed elsewhere this time. On the menu were Brahms' *Academic Festival* Overture and Debussy's *Fêtes* from his *Nocturnes*.

Brahms was familiar to me, but the Debussy was a new discovery, and I was bowled over by what amazing music this was. I loved learning it so much that I spent all my time on it. I stupidly neglected the Brahms, meaning that it wasn't in my head and soul enough, and therefore not in my arms and hands. Mr Grump made a surprise appearance, but he hadn't looked at either piece at all it seemed, and this didn't help with our teacher's sense of goodwill. He rightfully told us off in strict terms and after that didn't seem interested in working on our technique, or even sharing experiences or discussing interpretation. We all left slightly deflated.

I was thinking back to the times with my American piano teacher Alan in Utrecht, the endless talks about different styles and emotions, historic performances, the weekends at his house, the croissants and Bonzo. I was feeling a bit homesick, missing that particular aspect during my postgraduate studies here, when it had been our oxygen back in Holland.

We walked up to the Director's boardroom, as our masterclass was followed by lunch with Sir Colin Davis. Sir Colin was there to conduct Beethoven 9 with the college orchestra and even though we had hoped we'd be able to have a lesson with him, the college had organised light refreshments instead.

In the intimidating company of 'could-have-been Horowitz', this was still at least a chance to talk. And for the first time this year, almost like my lament had been heard, it was not about how to wave your arms (which didn't seem to interest him in the slightest), but just about the music. Celebrating this most epic of symphonies, which shook off historic convention and paved the way for all that followed. What it stood for, what it could mean to anyone, what it meant to us, and how differently great conductors had performed it over the centuries.

I found Sir Colin Davis to be a sombre man. He felt quite reserved and a bit distant in his manner with us. But his description of the opening of the Symphony, in just a few words and images, was incredibly vivid and clear and taught me more about the Symphony than many years of listening and watching it had done. At the end of our very English lunch – cucumber sandwiches (yet another first, and still not convinced) and elderflower cordial – he stood up, turned to Horowitz and said, suddenly quite excited, 'You know, we should plan an hour of conducting with these guys, before the first rehearsal with the college orchestra.' This threw Horowitz, but not even he could refuse this suggestion with the man standing there, clearly keen to make it happen. So, he agreed and told us to look out for a note with the timings in our mailboxes.

Perhaps not surprisingly, that note never appeared. When I asked him about it a while later, he just mumbled something like 'it was never going to work', and that was the end of it. It was another huge disappointment, but at least the great man's vision of the opening of the Symphony was there with the cucumber sandwiches, and I have used it many times during my own rehearsals.

I was able to watch that week's rehearsals. To my surprise there was a lot of talking and trying again, but the orchestra sounded great by the end.

Mr Grump never returned to college after that day, and we haven't seen each other since. It was back to score reading and analysis for me, and double portions of it.

Once a year a very wealthy Royal Opera House benefactor bought up all the top price seats at Covent Garden and offered them to music college students for very little. Bernard Haitink was coming to the end of his first full *Ring Cycle* in London, and these were tickets for the last instalment of it, the *Götterdämmerung*.

My better half and I had never seen a full Wagner opera live, let alone this epic finale to the *Ring Cycle*, so we got up early, making sure we wouldn't miss out on the opportunity. It was over four hours of drama, be it with a lengthy dinner break in the middle (awfully civilised, how it would have been done in Walhalla itself I would imagine). Great singers of the day adorned this performance. Anne Evans, John Tomlinson, Kurt Rydl to name but a few, and the orchestra were at their absolute peak under Haitink.

The production had caused lots of criticism, not least from Haitink himself, but I really loved it. It was clear, you knew who was who (which is crucial in this complicated plot with so many different characters), and at times it was very funny. In between the barer and more cartoon-like episodes, there were moments of staging that took your breath away by being powerful and atmospheric. The coming down of the massive cardboard box wall, exposing the burning Walhalla, was one of the most impressive pieces of operatic staging I have ever seen. Siegfried's funeral march had been crushing, with Haitink himself clearly deeply moved.

Those four hours flew by, and the final scene, with Brunhilde walking into the flames to her demise, covering her face with the shield as if to hide the shame of everything that had unfolded, had me in tears. Totally unexpectedly so. I don't cry in concerts!

The final melodies faded away to those closing chords. The world starting again. The feeling of that moment has never left me, and when I think back to it, tears well up again. I learned that I am a sentimental soul after all. And little did I know that this was just the start of a much bigger Royal *Ring Cycle* adventure...

At college my last big project involved auditions for the assistant conductorship of the Bournemouth Symphony Orchestra. Initially reserved just for students at my college, this was the first year it had been open to all conducting students in the UK. Bummer! It offered a great opportunity though, working closely with the orchestra's principal and guest conductors and bringing the possibility of conducting the orchestra itself (although this last element was very vague and not at all assured).

Living in Bournemouth or Poole for a year was another matter though. I had come to London to experience the best there was in the world and be in this centre of international life. One aspect to weigh up and to consider seriously.

The auditions were due to take place after college had finished, but we could start working on the music during the last few weeks of term. The repertoire was quite mainstream, Brahms' First Symphony and Rimsky-Korsakov's *Scheherazade*. But both pieces come with real challenges. There are many starts and stops in the middle movements of the *Scheherazade*, and the opening of the finale of the Brahms is an infamous nightmare to get right, let alone to give any 'interpretation' in the process.

Mr Grump had disappeared totally by now, and college was getting very quiet because of summer trips, tours and festivals. So, it was mainly me and my theory teacher working together and using the lessons to prepare as well as I could. Apart from the musical and technical work, it was also a great opportunity to talk with him about the past year and the future. He was a very wise man, quietly so, and I think an amazing conductor if he had been given the chance.

Our talks were about personalities, and that mysterious thing 'sound': how conductors get it, and how some don't, even if they talk about it at great length in rehearsals. Sound alone can hold emotion. Karajan was maybe the most famous creator of this, but Haitink was a master as well, and pianists like Artur Rubinstein and Sergei Rachmaninoff. They needed to do little with special effects, as their sound carried so much in itself. How to learn it, how to teach it, is one of the great fascinations of this amazing world of music making.

We also talked about how Mr Grump showed that just having a beautiful beat doesn't mean that people will want to play for you. As I was to find out, it is a constant judging of characters, and with that, a careful judging of methods. In an instant you must excel at problem spotting, solution finding and then being able to show it, and not just talk about it. Haitink told me later that his own shyness helped him greatly, as it forced him to show most things with his conducting itself, to avoid verbal confrontation.

I decided to throw all my Dutch directness, and garlic, at the college management, by asking for the opportunity to organise a final concert of the season and put *Scheherazade* on the programme. Probably scared of bad post-course reviews, the Director was keen to give the green light, and he even reserved the main concert hall for us and created rehearsal windows. Horowitz just sat there, mumbling that I would never find enough players to do it. Sadly, for him, the players were all very keen, as this is an important repertoire piece and a tough one with it. So, to be able to rehearse and perform it was a great chance for them to prepare for their own auditions in the future.

Not only did I manage to put an orchestra together, but they were also some of the star students at the college, and people I now see playing in top orchestras in the UK and beyond. The rehearsals were great fun, in very positive spirits, and even if I say so myself, it all sounded really good. For me to put into practice what I had decided to beat, and have the chance to adjust if needed, was a great position to be in. My teacher would come to the rehearsals and discuss things with me afterwards.

Literally three days before the concert, however, I got a message saying that sadly the concert hall was no longer available. Horowitz had decided to plan an end of year reception, at that time, in that hall. It transpired that, only weeks earlier, he had asked an ex-pupil to conduct the chamber orchestra for a radio broadcast, sweeping us aside. This had really angered me, especially after the Beethoven debacle. I had written an incensed letter to the Director about Horowitz's seeming sabotage of our course and opportunities, and questioning if they should have a course at all if clearly the students were not given anything to conduct.

It was lovely meeting with my Scandinavian violinist friend one last time, as she had also complained that none of the players on her postgraduate orchestral course had been invited to go on the orchestral tour to France. There was the now familiar white faux leather sofa, 'our' leather sofa almost, in the dark-brown tiled waiting room. We reminisced about the year and talked about our plans ahead. It was a good and warm moment, sadly halted by the Assistant Director calling me in to discuss the situation. He offered tea, probably as a preventative remedy, and seemed to have prepared for this particular occasion.

What followed was a monologue of apologetic-ness. He took a long time explaining the set-up of the course, regretting that they couldn't do more for us. But then he unexpectedly went further by making the hall available to us on the original date, and moving Horowitz's reception to the smaller recital hall, and to the evening. I was truly surprised and grateful, and I think I showed that sufficiently to him. He just seemed very relieved that this was the last time he had to face me and ushered me out of the office.

I would see my violinist friend again at the concert, but for the meantime, I wished her good luck as she was called in next. I never knew if she managed to get herself and her colleagues onto the tour... I suspect not... but hopefully they at least were offered cucumber sandwiches and a chat with the leader of the LSO.

I walked into the main corridor and saw Horowitz stomping towards me, a vision of great angry beard-ness. 'I don't like it when people say I don't do my job well!' he barked at me. 'I am sorry to hear that', I remember replying. 'Clearly your English is not up to scratch, calling me pretentious, when you meant prestigious, or something!' he screamed. I just looked at him and he walked off.

Horowitz climbed up the managerial ladder in the years to come and even made it to Deputy Head of the college, at least saving the world from him living out his legendary pianist career. Hopefully he had less direct powers, but instead just served more lunches and elderflower cordial to the students. All that mattered was that the concert had been saved.

Family and friends travelled from Holland to London to see it. The orchestra's playing was of a high level and for me to be able to guide them all through as I had hoped made for a proud and emotional final moment of my year here. Even though I would return for some lessons and projects, this was really it as far as the course went. And the college even gave me a prize!

The big, exciting, but also scary world of 'trying to make it as a conductor' was now lying ahead, but that was for later. For now, tea just would not do. There was much wine.

Scheherazade

On 27 February 1887, Alexander Borodin, doctor and chemist first, musician and composer second, attended a ball at the Medical and Surgical Academy in St Petersburg. Having suffered health problems his whole life, this proved one party too many and he dropped dead of a heart attack at the end

of the evening.

Borodin had been the most prominent member of the 'Mighty Five', a group of composers (Alexander Borodin, César Cui, Modeste Mussorgsky, Mily Balakirev and Nikolai Rimsky-Korsakov) whose aim was to create true Russian music, and he was seen as one of the leading musical voices of the day.

The group worked together in St Petersburg from 1856 until 1870, and it was Rimsky-Korsakov who saw it as his task to look after the legacy of his fellow composers the most. When Mussorgsky, a severe alcoholic, died in 1881 at only 42 years old, Rimsky-Korsakov made it his quest not only to preserve his music, but also to enhance and finish it when needed. The *Night on a Bare Mountain* was almost completely rewritten, something not all critics have been convinced by. Going back to the original, you can hear that Mussorgsky had a much darker sound in mind, but the reconstructed version by Rimsky-Korsakov has now become one of Mussorgsky's most celebrated works.

A similar thing happened that fateful night of the party at the Medical and Surgical Academy. Almost immediately after hearing the news of Borodin's death, Rimsky-Korsakov rushed to Borodin's apartment to save his music, and when he was there, he discovered the unfinished opera, *Prince Igor*. And like with Mussorgsky's music, he set out to rescue it from oblivion, and in the process turn it into Borodin's foremost masterpiece for posterity to behold.

And so, Rimsky-Korsakov worked hard throughout the winter of 1888 to finish the opera. It was set in ancient times, on wild Russian steppes and filled with exotic, powerfully passionate music. As his musical style was much closer to Borodin's than it had been to Mussorgsky's, the blend was almost seamless this time.

It seems no coincidence though that very shortly after completing *Prince Igor*, Rimsky-Korsakov started composing that big orchestral suite filled with exotic and passionate music of his own, based on the famous tale of the *Arabian Nights* (also known as *One Thousand and One Nights*). Rimsky-Korsakov's years at sea as a member of the Imperial Russian Navy would certainly have helped fuel his imagination. He named it *Scheherazade*, after one of the main characters, and it was to become arguably his most famous work. As he put it himself:

> *The programme I had been guided by consisted of separate, unconnected episodes of 'Arabian Nights', scattered through my suite. The Sea and Sinbad's Ship, the fantastic tale of Prince Kalendar, the Prince and the Princess, and finally the Baghdad Festival and the Ship dashing against the rock with the bronze knight on top of it.*
>
> *All I desired was that the listener should carry away the impression that it is an 'oriental' narrative of some numerous and varied fairytale wonders, and not just four pieces played one after the other.*

Love is the common theme throughout the story of the *Arabian Nights*, and the third movement of *Scheherazade* shows Rimsky-Korsakov at his most lyrical and musically intimate.

Not everywhere was this show of personal tenderness appreciated though. The very prudish English press of the day debated whether the famous repeated scale passage in the woodwind did in fact depict kissing. Could one imagine such a thing?! In the concert hall?! The criticism was fierce, and maybe this explained why Rimsky-Korsakov was hesitant to reveal too much detail about the exact sources of his inspiration.

The work has at its heart the famous violin solo. It is both seductive and impressive, embodying Scheherazade herself, and a real challenge for even the greatest of violinists. But there are huge soloistic demands everywhere, both for individual players as well as for the full orchestral sections. This is a massive 'listen to me and look at me' orchestral celebration, and with that, flexibility in its musical flow is crucial. Giving time for the solos to unfold the way the individual players want them to, and then bringing that same flexibility to the matching sections for the whole orchestra. Call it orchestral rubato maybe, like one huge symphonic song.

On top of that, it seems to be a maze of starts and stops, especially in the *Prince Kalendar* movement. And here it demonstrates that it is a piece that truly puts the conductor through their paces. Often, a conductor will struggle, forcing the players to find their own path in the face of their clumsy directions, rather than giving the players freedom by being the guide on the rostrum who knows the way.

I think that my years as a flautist really helped me in these musical situations. In the end, it is all about breathing. The upbeat that 'takes-in' the air, which the players can then breathe out as sound. And that 'preparing moment' can sometimes fall on a downbeat, requiring us also to be very clear where we are in the bar. Once the 'breathing-in' finds its way to the conductor's hands and arms (and baton, if used), suddenly everything seems much simpler, and everybody is able to 'sing' together. And of course, the results are never the same, that is the whole point. It is life itself.

I have lived through many different recordings of *Scheherazade*, but the one I keep coming back to is Leopold Stokowski with the London Symphony Orchestra (LSO). Of all conductors, Stokowski managed the most to get that freedom of phrasing and flexibility of rubato out of any orchestra he conducted.

The amusing tale that he was born Leo Stokes and changed his name to sound Russian has now been shown to be false. But he was known to put on a thick Russian accent, even though he was born and raised in London's Marylebone. And he was not shy to give his birthdate as seven years later than it actually was. The rumours of a name change were true though for his first wife, Lucy Mary Agnes Hickenlooper, from Galveston, Texas. When her piano career didn't take off as planned, she decided to change her name to Olga Samaroff, with the desired effect. She urged her husband to do the same and focus purely, and at times theatrically, on his Eastern European roots.

Watching Stokowski shape orchestral playing with his movements, from his shoulders to his fingertips, is like watching magic happen. He is able to create pauses mid-flow somehow, and every single player is held in the same musical breath. For me his recordings of *La Mer* and *Prélude à l'après midi d'un faune* are still unrivalled, as is the way he folds the Philadelphia Orchestra around Rachmaninoff's piano playing in the composer's own piano concertos. And like the greatest, he could unleash huge emotional depth in sound.

All this suits *Scheherazade* perfectly and the fairytale dreams come to life in the most intoxicating way. Stokowski made no fewer than six recordings of the work, and each one has its own merits, but the 1974 version with the LSO seems to have it all. It makes any other attempt, even the benchmark ones by Beecham, Monteux and the more manic Gergiev, sound a little wooden and clumsy in comparison. Karajan possibly comes closest, but just lacks that seductive flirtatious quality that Stokowski gives us.

Rimsky-Korsakov died in 1908 at the age of 64. He had become one of the country's foremost musicians, leaving towering orchestral works like the *Capriccio Espagnole*, *Easter* Overture and of course *Scheherazade*, as well as sixteen operas. He was a master of orchestration and shaped a generation of younger composers and musicians through the decades of dedicated teaching he undertook. And whilst his own style was closest to that of his friends Balakirev and Borodin, he guided young Russian composers like Prokofiev and Stravinsky to a much more modern idiom. And people like Ravel, Debussy and Respighi were undeniably influenced by his artistry.

Most of us though will probably remember him for the *Flight of the Bumblebee*, that tiny little bit of instrumental acrobatics from his rarely performed opera *The Tale of Tsar Saltan.*

He would have accepted that happily. Rimsky-Korsakov didn't seem to take his own standing too seriously.

> *'What could be more intolerable than ritual? I feel positively embarrassed when I attend them, like acting out a comedy, even at funerals. Yet I have had so much fun, depicting them in my music! I believe that art is essentially the most fascinating and intoxicating of lies!'*
> *Nikolai Rimsky-Korsakov*

Name dropping

> ***'Imagination creates reality.'***
> *Richard Wagner*

Prometheus seems to have had it in for The Royal Opera House at Covent Garden, as the famous music temple we know today is the third theatre that was built on that spot.

The first opened its doors in 1732, its location roughly the same as today and having been the gardens of a convent before that. Mainly there to host plays, it sadly burnt to the ground in 1808. It was hastily rebuilt, in a design by Robert Smirke, a name that always puts one on my face. The spelling is not quite accurate, but still...

In 1843, the Theatre Act ended the monopoly held by certain theatres to perform dramatic works, and suddenly music and opera made their way to what was now named the Theatre Royal. The company taking residence was given the title the 'Royal Italian Opera'. It seems hard to imagine that going down well in our current Brexit times. And maybe it also annoyed our God of Fire, because for a second time, in 1856, the theatre was destroyed by flames.

Enter the Lucas Brothers. Not a famous group of young musicians from the *Disney Channel*, or hunky Australian actors, but two respected British architects of the time, and they built the theatre that pretty much still stands today. The Company was dutifully renamed the 'Royal English Opera Company' (the title, of course, makes sense, but seems a bit disappointing somehow). It was only a small step from that to the 'Royal Opera at Covent Garden'.

After a big renovation in the 1990s, 'The House' as it is affectionately known, looks even more awe-inspiring, but it was already breathtaking. Those red velvet seats, golden balconies and boxes and decorative woodwork, that heavenly painted ceiling: it really took my breath away when I first visited for that *Götterdämmerung*. In Holland I had never experienced a theatre like this, so full of historic splendour. The Amsterdam

Stopera is a modern theatre, and we're always reminded that its salmon pink carpet was indeed a risky choice for a venue where night after night lots of people tread in from the street.

Here I was at Covent Garden, sitting in the empty auditorium watching an orchestral rehearsal for *Siegfried*, the third opera preceding the *Götterdämmerung* in Wagner's *Ring Cycle*. Bernard Haitink at the helm, with me sitting just behind his highly respected assistant David Syrus on the front row of the stalls. Syrus had just given me a pocket score, to be able to follow the music in detail. But for me, just seeing the rehearsal take shape and watching the great conductor at work with his beloved orchestra was at that point more important than following things note by note.

Haitink was not a man of many words in his rehearsals, and he steered the orchestra through the first Act without stopping. It turned out that this was the only time the orchestra had a chance to play through the opera without singers and stage. This was, and still is, the UK way. Minimum rehearsals, much to the frustration of many of the musicians involved. Haitink put his baton down and thought for a bit. Then he just said, 'This music is so spectacular, but also there is so much tenderness and wittiness, we should make a lot more effort to bring out the quiet and subtle sides. Not too loud, not too loud... Let's try again.' Which they did.

This time, it was not just good playing, but something much greater happened. Haitink's baton became a sorcerer's wand, from which the desired sound was sent, as if by magic, to the players who greedily picked it up and made it their own.

And that sound became 'one' (I don't know how else to describe it), and with a silvery shine. Little pauses and rubato moments suddenly appeared without explanation or any verbal request.

At one point the woodwind and brass were not quite together on a crucial chord. Haitink stopped. He smiled and asked politely if they could try that again. There was another messy arrival, and Haitink suddenly seemed slightly annoyed. I remember him saying, 'I think I am as clear as I can be, but if there is anything else I can do to help to get this point absolutely together, do let me know.' The section looked slightly shocked but also disappointed with themselves. They nailed it at the third go, and every single time after that. The magic and 'being one' was restored.

We had come to the rehearsal break, and behind me someone was carrying a little fold-up table with two chairs, placing them in the middle of the auditorium. Haitink took some time to talk about musical details with David Syrus and then went to the table, which now had tea and sandwiches on it, and gestured for me to join him. I was unsure if I should. Surely, he wouldn't have lunch with the Dutch student he had only met once before. But he waved again, and there I found myself, sitting under a dome of gold, surrounded by a sea of red velvet, talking to one of the greatest conductors of our time.

He asked me if I liked the music, and how I felt about that specific opera as part of the whole *Ring Cycle*. I must have blurted out some vague compliments and ramblings, but bit by bit I relaxed through Haitink's kind and warm manner. He would never talk about music in pretentious academic terms, but always in a way that made total sense and related very directly to the emotions of it. I remember he took some time to find the right word to describe the opera. 'Difficult' was the word he chose, which made me smile.

Siegfried is indeed a very difficult opera, being the scherzo movement of the cycle. It is very funny at times, but also full of high drama, a lot of complex plotlines and highly psychological. On top of that, the orchestral score is fiendishly hard. In all of this, clarity is key – and something that Haitink had mastered completely.

The conversation turned to conducting in general. To hear the great man talk about his 'job' as he called it, his/our responsibilities as a conductor and finding a way to enable the players to play at their absolute best, was not only a huge inspiration, but also really moving. It seemed to me that he felt as the conductor, you are, above all, there to serve the musicians. Serve first of all with that clarity, something which kept coming back over the times I spent with him working on specific pieces. Always make sure everyone knows where they are and what is going on, as this creates freedom for them to reach for the deepest level of music making, sharing of emotion and trying to really bring across what the composer intended.

For Haitink, the woodwind and brass would often play too loud. This was something that got him into trouble at times with certain players, especially in his early years in Amsterdam. He had that great way of making a point, in simple short sentences. 'Always so loud, always so loud, why?' I remember him saying. Balancing of levels, both dynamically and emotionally: that was what stood out for me from that particular conversation. Build up and judge where the big emotional outbursts need to be. He was very open in saying that conducting opera had helped him a lot to perfect the creation of emotional arcs.

He shared some funny anecdotes about the new aspects opera and ballet had brought to his conducting. Having to adapt the speed of a ballet score to fit the 'jump time' a dancer would need, very much depending on the physicality of that particular dancer. And how often he would be confronted with a cast change at the very last minute, because with the realities of ballet, injuries lie just around the corner. Being all geared up for the speed of Miss A, but suddenly Miss B would appear on stage. No time to think, but immediately having to adapt to the new scenario.

It was clear he loved working at the Royal Opera House but struggled more with the business side of things. These were turbulent times for the company, with severe budget cuts and even threats of closure. But he always stood firm for his musicians and singers, even if it meant putting his own position on the line.

At the end of the break, he stood up and said, 'You know, more and more I believe a strong upbeat is really the key to most aspects of leading an orchestra. I am still surprised that many great musical minds don't have a strong upbeat, even after years and years of doing it!' His advice to me was to see as many conductors at work as possible, and to 'steal, steal, steal!' He gave me a big smile and a pat on the shoulder, and it was back to work. Back to Wagner's wonderful world of dragons, birds, heroes and foes. I was in a dreamlike state by now, but also determined to take all this wisdom and 'steal, steal, steal'.

I had come into contact with Haitink after sending a lot of letters to conductors that spring, asking them for advice and possibly a meeting. Letters seem so old fashioned now, but that was how things were done in those days. With the bible that was the *Musicians' Yearbook* on my desk, I found the names of their musical agents and picked the conductors who I admired as musicians and who seemed warm personalities. And a few because they fascinated me and showed support to younger conductors.

That included Haitink, an absolute hero of mine. But for me he was so above anyone else, and on such a hectic schedule conducting all over the world, that I knew there was little chance I would hear anything back. He did live in London however, and with him being at Covent Garden for longer stretches, I thought I would try anyway, and sent my letter directly to the Opera House.

I was surprised how many responses did come back. A lovely long letter from Jeffrey Tate, with an invite to meet him at his house in Camden. The funniest note from Vladimir Ashkenazy, which looked like it was written on the back of a napkin. Clearly in a rush, which made it even more generous, him still taking the time to reply and share his wisdom. Lawrence Foster, the American-Romanian conductor, who manages to coax the lushest sounds out of any orchestra he works with, phoned me up and spoke at length about the profession and great ways to get a foot in the door. He had already heard of me as I was about to conduct the Transylvanian State Philharmonic, an orchestra he had connections with. Learn music, see people at work ('steal, steal, steal'), try competitions and/or go down the opera repetiteur route: these were the outstanding pieces of advice.

A Dutch conductor working in Austria generously offered me an audition for a repetiteur position at the theatre where he was the Music Director. As it was a small provincial town, I decided not to take up the offer, and I will never know if that was the right decision. But I loved London, and being there was crucial to me then, especially as work was starting to come in bit by bit. It seemed too soon to leave.

I did meet with Jeffrey Tate at his beautiful mews house in Camden. Principal Conductor of the Rotterdam Philharmonic until the previous year, I had seen him conduct a lot. His technique seemed very natural to me, and his music making had a flow that was so inevitable that everybody appeared, instantaneously, to be on the same wavelength. In the end, his partnership with Rotterdam didn't work out, but for me he got some of the best sounds out of them. Their *Midsummer Night's Dream* and *Enigma Variations* are up there with the greatest. He was kind and personable, as he had seemed in interviews I'd watched.

I caught him rushing around the house packing suitcases, as he was about to embark on a concert tour of Europe. His partner was equally lovely and made the best coffee I had drunk in years. Tate took great interest in my story and told me all about his beginnings as an opera pianist and working his way through the German *Kapellmeister* system. It didn't surprise me, as his conducting was like making chamber music with colleagues, possibly something that wasn't always desired in Rotterdam.

He generously gave me contacts to write to at different opera houses, as a way to introduce myself into that world. For him, this seemed the best way to get started and to make full use of my piano and opera skills. His taxi to Heathrow arrived and he apologised for having to leave, but he told me not to rush, and finish my (now third) cup of coffee, which I did. His partner kindly let me out and I walked back to the Tube with a lot to think about when it came to which direction to take for my next steps.

And then in the autumn, the letter landed on the doormat. The name on the back was an unclear scribble, so I opened it and started reading. It was in Dutch and handwritten. 'Please forgive me for not replying sooner', it said. 'I have been very busy and only now have had the time to catch up with my correspondence.' I quickly looked for the name at the bottom. 'Yours, Bernard Haitink.' I just couldn't believe it, and the adrenaline started to rush through my system. I read through the letter again. 'If you would not mind that I might have to cancel last minute, then do please come and see me at my house, as I am now in London for a longer period of time. Do ring me, best after 4pm, and this is my address...' It left me totally speechless.

I picked up the phone at 3:45pm, after hours of nervous 'should I, shouldn't I?'. I dialled the number and was greeted by a friendly female voice. I explained who I was, rattling in double speed, with her having to ask me a few times to slow down. And then came a slightly stern reprimand, 'you were asked to phone after 4, it is still before! I will call my husband, but next time, don't ring too soon as it is his resting time.' I gulped and made a mental note.

Haitink sounded cheerful and relaxed, and quickly waved away my grovelling apology for the timing of the call, assuring me that he was already in his afternoon schedule. His manner immediately put me at ease and made me lose all my nerves. After a short conversation, we arranged to meet at his house that Friday.

It turned out that he lived only a 15-minute walk away, in South Kensington. The house wasn't huge, but it was beautiful, its location perfect, in a quiet and very green little hideaway just a few minutes from the Tube station. Black and white floor tiles led me up to the front door. His warm handshake and smile when he greeted me made me feel welcome straight away. 'Come in, come in, it is so wonderful to finally meet you, and apologies again it took me so long to reply to your letter, the summer has been crazy.'

I remember the bright orange sofa, the Bechstein grand piano which he invited me to play (my mind blanking, but some clumsy Rachmaninoff coming out), and his extensive CD collection. Ranging from old Furtwängler and Karajan recordings to solo piano music, Andras Schiff clearly a favourite. There was just one CD of his own recording of a Mahler symphony. It sat there almost apologetically.

He told me he lamented that he himself was not a good pianist, as it was great thing for a conductor. 'I was just a mediocre string player', he laughed, probably underselling his talents wildly. 'Can I entice you with a cup of coffee? We can sit out on the terrace.'

I wandered into the kitchen with him. It was bold red, more black and white tiles, and had beautiful work surfaces. His handling of the coffee machine was as expert as his conducting of Bruckner. We went out to the terrace, which was raised above the back garden. In the warm autumn sun and with the dome of the Catholic Cathedral as the backdrop, it felt like being in Rome.

He took all the time to talk to me, enthusiastically sharing his own experiences. His parting from the Concertgebouw Orchestra wasn't that long ago, and it was clearly something that still weighed heavily on his mind and soul. He talked freely about personalities in the orchestra, and the tough years he'd had being a young chief conductor in Amsterdam. They didn't spare him it seemed, and it was something that had never quite left him. He spoke like someone who was not at all awestruck by his own standing and fame. He was completely personable and 'equal' in his tone, interested in my story and showing a huge willingness, eagerness really, to help if he possibly could.

It was then that he first talked about the importance of a strong and clear upbeat. And how clarity meant freedom. He told me how he had seen a conductor insisting on not beating at all during a mysteriously quiet section of a contemporary composition. The players kept getting the timing wrong, and the leader asked if they could get a firm downbeat. The conductor said that that would ruin the atmosphere. But his vague gestures had the opposite effect, making the players actually play louder in an attempt to find clarity for themselves. 'I prefer being clear, and then invite the players to play as quietly as possible, it gives them the ability to do so somehow.'

This was followed by his humorous recollections of being pigeonholed as 'safe and boring' by some of the press in Holland. 'You know, I would think to myself: let them have it, I am really going for it tonight, being almost overly emotional and expressive. And afterwards, I would feel exhausted, but also like I had surely cracked it this time. But the review would come, again saying it was a solid and safe performance. You just can't win sometimes. And I learned to just trust my own judgment, and my musicians' judgments – most of the time, at least!' Followed by loud laughter.

After nearly two hours, he apologised for needing to finish our meeting, as he was preparing for rehearsals at Covent Garden. The full run of the *Ring Cycle*, which was taking place over the next few months. That same production of which we had seen the *Götterdämmerung*, and with a dream cast of singers. He said he'd think about what he could do to help and apologised for not being able to offer concrete conducting opportunities. He lamented that in the current climate, even his recommendations about young conductors he knew well, and rated highly, were not taken very seriously. But he had decided that it would be good for me to come and watch as many Wagner rehearsals as possible at Covent Garden in the following weeks (at which my mouth dropped), and he would be very happy to work on specific pieces, if I wanted to. 'Not lessons!' he said, 'but maybe just exploring music sessions, or something', calling it 'advice'. As long as I didn't mind if he had to cancel at the last minute. Like I would!

His generosity was beyond what I had dared to hope for, and I thanked him profusely, falling back into my garbling style. He stopped me mid-sentence and told me my rehearsal pass would be waiting for me on Monday morning at the stage door, something he had clearly already organised. And he invited me to meet at his house again in a few weeks, maybe with a video recording of my conducting, but definitely with my baton and the score of Brahms 1, which I was preparing for the Bournemouth audition later that month and had asked him about. Especially the start of that last movement.

It was getting dark, and the street lanterns had lit up. A touch of wintery cold infused the evening breeze. 'Isn't it atmospheric? I love London' he said. I remember replying that it was straight out of a Dicken's novel, which made him smile. A quick wave, and he closed the door. I walked back to our tiny shoebox of a flat, but it felt like I was floating on air.

I remember Haitink saying towards the end of that first meeting that being a conductor can be quite lonely. In his experience, a lot of conductors were not very supportive of each other. As he put it, 'There are a lot of difficult personalities out there, sometimes I think that as a breed we are not very sympathetic.'

We know of some amazing tales of course. Toscanini famously kicking over music stands and smashing his baton on one of them – or was it even on the head of a first viola player? And I once saw Romanian conductor Celibidache tell off his first flute player with wild gestures, on stage, during a performance of Ravel's *Bolero*. And then continuing to do so after it had finished, whilst people were applauding.

But I could never have imagined how Haitink's insight into conductors' personalities, and those Wagner rehearsals, would result in me playing a small part in denying a grand diva of the operatic stage one of her last main concert opportunities.

Monday morning and Covent Garden was busy as always. Commuter crowds were fighting to get through the tiny Tube station, and the market was packed with tourists. Street performers doing their thing, musicians and singers busking, this was already very much like a chorus scene from an opera.

The lady at the stage door seemed to be expecting me, and handed me my red rehearsal pass, signed by Haitink. I clutched it tightly and walked into the building, for the start of the next chapter of my life in London.

This was to become my world for the next six weeks, teaching me just about everything I know about conducting, and getting a unique glimpse of what it takes to bring Wagner's monumental *Ring Cycle* to life. The dedication of everyone involved and the almost superhuman efforts of the singers. The funny moments, but also the very serious and tense moments. I was totally sucked-in to the journey everyone was on, and which somehow interweaved with the *Cycle* itself.

I sneaked into the auditorium. Haitink was talking to David Syrus, and I didn't want to disturb him. But Haitink saw me, said hello and offered me a seat next to Syrus, just behind the pit. He apologised for not having more time to talk, as it was straight in with that morning's stage and orchestra rehearsal for *Das Rheingold*. The journey started here.

As the production schedule was impossibly tight, the stage rehearsals that followed were all about fixing only what needed fixing urgently. There was very little stopping and starting.

Everyone knew their stuff and was aware there was very limited time to be able to try things out, let alone mess up.

At times, Haitink would address the orchestra during playing, giving clear instructions mainly about balance and articulation. He had this incredible 'stare' he could throw at a section when demanding precision, and a whole repertoire of subtle gestures, signals almost, that left no doubt as to what was noted and needed attention. Tuning, balance, rhythmical tightness: he never allowed sloppiness to kick in. But he would also enable the musicians to breathe, and put their stamp on the performance, taking a woodwind solo for instance and accommodating for musical space if needed. Nothing was set in stone; it all came together as the playing unfolded and as he had talked about. His own clarity was there to set the artistry free. The singers rarely faltered, but inevitably a few times things became slightly unstuck and had to be done again.

The atmosphere was friendly and warm, except when in Haitink's eyes time was being wasted. In this production, the two giants, Fasolt and Fafner, shared one enormous pair of trousers and had three legs between them. Combine this with a stage that was severely sloped, and it was clear that moving around became incredibly hard. One particular movement, where they had to turn quickly at the back of the stage, resulted without fail in the giants accidently falling over and then sliding down the slope. Several attempts were made, but to no avail. Everyone on stage was cracking up, not managing to keep a straight face. It was at these moments of silliness that Haitink would seldom join in, but rather became quite strict, and, politely, but with a tone of severity, call class to order. The only exception was the pumpkin head of the Dragon in *Siegfried* that kept falling off. Not even Haitink could hold back his laughter, the weeks of intense concentration needing an outlet perhaps. He called for a short break to have the crucial body part reattached, and it behaved for the rest of the afternoon.

As with the orchestral session, the singers and orchestra all started to become one, just in the process of going through the music. Haitink's total mastery of the score and ability to give every singer their cue when needed very much made this happen. He would always allow for breathing, and dramatic time when necessary, and made the orchestra follow seamlessly. At times David Syrus would give specific vocal instructions, mainly about clarity of diction. The Stage Director only once or twice interrupted the rehearsal, giving his notes mostly in the breaks. This was often to make sure the singers were pointing the right way for us to hear their every word.

This production was a revival, and for most people it was about fine-tuning and adapting to small changes made from previous years. Hardly ever did a rehearsal overrun, and if so, only by minutes. Often Haitink tried to finish a little early, knowing that rest was essential for everyone to be able to perform again, often that same evening. And it was that strict 'no time wasting' that allowed for him to do so.

I became a bit naughty and decided to test if the rehearsal pass would also get me into the opera performances, and it turned out that it did, most of the time. Standing at the back of the stalls, it was incredible to see the rehearsals transform into the real thing, with the audience 'tension' and dramatic continuity.

I still can't believe how Haitink could conduct a three (or more) hour-long rehearsal of *Götterdämmerung* during the day, and then go straight into *Die Walküre* that same evening, repeating the same pattern most days each week. His conducting technique was incredibly efficient, and a lot of the strength came from clear but economical movements. I started calling it the 'Haitink flick'. An upbeat that could set 100 people off into an emotional storm, whilst saving the total abandonment for the essential moments. It certainly allowed him to keep this crazy schedule without any loss of emotional or dramatic connection.

During the breaks in rehearsals, I would go into the artists' canteen where everyone was very generous with their time, and amazingly so. There was a true team spirit, and lots and lots of food being consumed. Energy, and more energy. I could ask the singers questions and talk to the repetiteurs about the job they did creating rich orchestral sounds from a piano, and they would all happily tell me their many stories. And so the weeks passed, and I absorbed (and now realise, 'stole, stole, stole'), with those *Siegfried* tea breaks proving to be the most magical of times.

Imitating the 'Haitink flick' is still a powerful weapon for me in making things go the way they should, or in pulling back the ranks when a slight unravelling threatens to creep in. And his *subito piano* gesture is worth its weight in gold, being effective every time. Even the slight squinting of the eyes as to ask, 'was that quite right?' No need to raise my voice, ever!

During that time, I had also written to a guest conductor of one of London's main orchestras. It had been quite a while, but to my surprise, his agent suddenly phoned up to say he wanted to meet me during a rehearsal that week.

That morning, there had been a long stage and orchestra session at the Opera House. One of the smaller parts was being sung by an ageing singer, once of decent fame, but now struggling vocally. It was a bit sad to hear, especially as the rest of the cast was astounding. She got through it, but only just.

Afterwards, I rushed across town for my meeting with the guest Maestro. I arrived just before the rehearsal was about to start and had a quick chat with one of the French horn players, who I happened to know from college. He was expressing his concern about the lack of communication in Maestro's conducting, and the orchestra had struggled to cope with his unexpected changes of tempo in performance. I was intrigued, and sat down at the back of the auditorium, watching Maestro rehearse. He stopped a lot and seemed to be talking more than letting the orchestra play. In the break his agent waved in my direction and directed me to his dressing room.

Maestro was sitting behind the grand piano, playing through sections of the symphony, and said nothing. After about five minutes of awkwardness, I decided to break the silence, hoping he wouldn't kick me out for interrupting his playing. A quick hello, and he then told me how he had injured his left shoulder. But because of his amazing ability, he could still make the orchestra do exactly what he wanted, 'as opposed to so many conductors who couldn't even make them play properly with both arms fully functioning!', he said. I felt a bit uneasy after hearing the complete opposite from the horn player earlier, but thought I'd better not bring that up.

After ten minutes of him talking about his own career, the agent flew into the room with the bad news that the soloist for the song cycle the following evening had called in sick and cancelled. With me still present, the search for a replacement started there and then.

'How about Miss A?', the agent asked. 'Ah no, she is very close to Claudio Abbado and he is such a fraud!' replied the Maestro. Ouch, the gloves were clearly coming off, and as a self-confessed superfan of Abbado (one of the greatest conductors of our time), it was hard for me not to stage a verbal intervention at that point. 'Or Mr B?' asked the agent. 'No, he won't do. He is so full of himself!' came the reply. 'Well, how about Miss C? She might be in the late summer of her career, but still has a fabulous voice...' Wait, she was the singer I had heard that morning at the Wagner rehearsal! 'No, no', the Maestro exclaims. 'She is surely past it vocally!'

The agent now tries his best to change the Maestro's mind, as Miss C really is the last available option. The Maestro suddenly turns to me and asks, 'have you heard her sing recently?' I couldn't believe it, but admitted that I had seen her rehearse that very morning. 'Was she any good?' he asked. Put on the spot like that, my train of thought wavered. I could hear myself saying that I wasn't completely impressed, but it being the first rehearsal, maybe...

The Maestro cuts me off, turns to the agent and says, 'I told you so, we'd better find someone else.' The agent promptly left the dressing room, tail between his legs. Did that just happen?

The rehearsal then started again. I stayed for a bit of the second half, bemused that the Maestro kept turning around mid-music, proudly showing off how he managed to get the orchestra to slow down. With just one arm!

I sneaked out and to this day feel guilty that I, just out of college and not in any position to judge, might have denied Miss C her song cycle. But that afternoon did make me realise that Haitink's words about our 'breed' came from many long years of experience. And at times now, I am reminded of them. We conductors are indeed a funny bunch.

The last weeks of rehearsals and performances at Covent Garden arrived. And with them, the towering challenge that is the *Götterdämmerung*: over four hours of drama, plot twists and intrigue that puts most soap operas and Hollywood blockbusters in the shade. The cast was the stuff of dreams. Deborah Polaski at her peak as Brunhilde. Siegfried Jerusalem, maybe in the autumn of his career, but still eternally youthful in his characterisation of Siegfried, and with more warmth vocally than I remember from earlier productions. Both were like naughty school kids between the scenes in rehearsal, giggling away and making stupid jokes. The drama of *Götterdämmerung* is so intense, it seemed to me that they needed to let off steam to be able to get back into the emotional onslaught of it all.

Funnily enough, Haitink made nothing of their joking around and happily left them to it. But I did see him lose his cool when the Woodbird missed her entrance for a third time, claiming not to be able to get up a ladder quickly enough to feel comfortable to sing. It was the only time in all those weeks that he properly snapped. But it was still very respectful.

During those last sessions, you could feel a sense from everyone of 'the story coming to an end'. A certain sadness almost, but also gratitude. I didn't manage to speak to Haitink after seeing my final rehearsal. I left him a long letter, trying to explain my feelings about this opportunity and truly life-enriching experience.

I sneaked into a performance later that week, now feeling close to the characters and the artists portraying them. The sound of the orchestra was rich and dark from the start. The magical scene with the Norns realising that the cords of rule and reason have snapped, and that the world is hurtling towards its inevitable demise. The hours flew by, and I was getting every detail and nuance of the story and its heroes and villains.

Siegfried's betrayal was even more brutally played out in this revival than before, and Brunhilde's treatment more humiliating. Their moments of fun had made the drama far stronger and hurtful. I remember Siegfried Jerusalem's last top note being of a beauty and intensity I hadn't heard before. You could feel everyone being overwhelmed by shock and grief during the Funeral March, Haitink finding even higher levels of intensity and musical power than before, and the orchestra seemed possessed almost. I have never experienced the immolation scene so truly crushing as sung then by Deborah Polaski. In total command vocally, she was able to capture all the anger, love, doubt, and ultimately an almost devastating determination. The wall collapsing again, Brunhilde walking into the flames of the burning Walhalla, enabling the world to start anew. (We did always think of those poor stagehands though, having to reassemble it, thousands of cardboard boxes, every day and every night...)

Those final melting melodic lines, with Haitink drawing them out as much as was physically possible, much more so than in the rehearsals, like threads towards eternity, and every player was with him completely.

The end came too soon, but then it was always going to.

Verdi vs Wagner

In 1889, by then aged 76, Verdi said that 'amongst my works I like best is the house I built in Milan, to house elderly singers.'

Around 25 years before, when arguably the most famous opera composer of all, he had become so financially independent that he was able to retire completely from composing. At this point he was one of the wealthiest people in Europe and had just received the equivalent of three million dollars for his latest opera, *Aida.*

Verdi's *Un ballo in maschera* had been my first proper foray into conducting opera, and it coincided with my time at the Royal Opera House watching and experiencing the *Ring Cycle.*

Together with Richard Wagner, Verdi was centre stage of the nineteenth century operatic world. Even though they never met in person, and didn't openly discuss each other's styles much, the feeling was that there was a lot of resentment between these two musical giants. However, it was never shown or expressed in a tone of conflict. This they left to the likes of Brahms and Tchaikovsky...

At the end of his life, Verdi said in an interview with a German newspaper that Wagner had been one of the greatest geniuses, who left treasures of immortal worth. As an Italian, he continued, he didn't understand everything, but before *Tristan and Isolde* he declared, 'I stand both in wonder and terror.'

Music was never Verdi's only passion. The politics he had always been so involved in, as well as philanthropy, became more and more important to him. So, after *Aida*, he decided to call it quits and leave composing behind. He fulfilled a longstanding wish to be a landowner and became very socially involved by organising many meals for the poor and taking on big humanitarian projects.

In interviews, he liked to indulge in describing the simple and impoverished upbringing he had experienced himself, but now it seems his descriptions were likely to have been exaggerated. His parents were very successful in the agricultural industry and keen to give little Guiseppe a high-quality musical education, at whatever cost. And it paid off, as soon he had worked his way up from Concert Master of the local orchestra to being possibly the most famous musician in the world.

His operas were performed everywhere. *Un ballo in maschera*, for example, travelled from Rome to Paris, via London, to the Metropolitan Opera in New York that same year of 1889. And this was no exception. His operas were particularly popular in the USA, where theatres had been putting on opera productions from as early as 1829. Initially criticised for being too dramatic and over the top, Verdi's works gained more and more respect, and soon were seen all over the New World.

Verdi had known huge tragedy in his personal life, when his young wife Margherita Barezzi died in 1840 following the deaths of all five of their children. It took him years to come back to public life and composing success, but in 1842, it was *Nabucco* that became his first major international hit, reaching opera houses as far afield as Buenos Aires.

Aida was commissioned nearly thirty years and 22 operas later by the Cairo Opera House, where it premiered to huge acclaim in 1871. Verdi himself wasn't there for the premiere, saying that he was 'scared to be mummified at arrival', a fate not much better than what he had bestowed upon poor Aida herself. Maybe he feared a curse.

He had found personal happiness again with the famous soprano Guiseppina Strepponi. They had remained unmarried for a very long time, but eventually the pressures of society, weighing heavier on Guiseppina than Guiseppe, made them decide to tie the knot. They were together until her death in 1897 aged 82, three years before his.

After several years of his self-inflicted retirement, Verdi couldn't resist the ever-mounting external pressure to return to composing. He came back with his last three masterpieces in a style that was developing dramatically.

Otello displayed an almost verismo style that reminds us of Puccini and Mascagni, who were only just starting to make names for themselves. Then there was the Requiem, and finally, *Falstaff*. For this, his last opera, Verdi switched musical direction again and through-composed the work: no separate recitatives and arias, but everything flowing forward in one long dramatic musical wave. And this suited another aspect that was new to him, using a comedic tale as a base. 'After having relentlessly massacred so many heroes and heroines, I can at least now have some fun with them' he commented, before taking on the challenge.

Verdi died eight years later, and his retirement home, *Casa Verdi* in Milan, still houses artists and musicians to this day.

After studying his subject for many years, Verdi's biographer John Rosselli wrote, 'I don't very much like the man Verdi, the autocratic rentier-come-estate owner, full time grumbler and reactionary critic. But a deep integrity runs beneath his life and can be felt even when he is being unreasonable or wrong.'

As a conductor and opera 'Musical Director', I was thrown in at the deep end with *Un ballo in maschera*, which falls in Verdi's middle period and was finally premiered in Rome in 1859.

I was very fortunate to experience, simultaneously, the totally different styles of Wagner and Verdi first hand. I could certainly hear how they had inspired each other, even though neither might have been happy to admit it.

The *Ballo* we know today is the result of numerous changes and rewrites, and almost certainly as many sleepless nights for Verdi and his text writer, Antonio Somma.

It all began when Verdi came across the original libretto by Eugène Scribe. It tells the story of the death of King Gustav III of Sweden at a masked ball in Stockholm in 1792 and was a bit of a chaotic mix between fact and fiction. Whilst the main players were real historical figures, such as King Gustav, Anckarström (the King's secretary and confidante) and Ulrika (a fortune teller, of course), there were also new characters and fictional aspects, such as the romance between Gustav and Anckarström's wife, Amelia. This affair was given as the reason for Gustav's murder, as opposed to Anckarström's personal hatred for the King.

Verdi and Somma began work on the new opera in 1857, tentatively calling it *Gustavo III*. However, many changes were demanded after its submission. The action should be in a pre-Christian era, the conspirators shouldn't be motivated by power, and most significantly, the character of Gustav should be changed.

Things then got even more complicated in January 1858, when an assassination attempt was made on Napoleon III in Paris by Felice Orsini and two other Italians, conspirators if you like. A new overhaul was promptly ordered, but a frustrated Verdi refused to make changes such as moving the action to fourteenth century Florence and giving it a new title. In the end, Verdi contested the issue in a commercial court and eventually the court ruled in his favour.

The next new version, re-named *Una vendetta in domino*, was sent to the Teatro Apollo in Rome. In the end, the only main change that was demanded was for the location to be switched to somewhere outside Europe. Boston was swiftly chosen, and with some different character names, the opera was now called *Un ballo in maschera*.

Another issue Verdi had to tackle was that Gustav III had been an openly gay ruler, and quite flamboyantly so. At the time, there was absolutely no option to include this as part of the story. Where he could, Verdi tried to suggest elements of it in the characters surrounding Gustavo (who was now called Riccardo), as well as in the dramatic circumstances. Finally, after two years of haggling and changing, the curtain went up, and came down again three hours later to rapturous applause. And the rest, as they say, is history.

Despite all the changes, *Un ballo in maschera* still comes together cohesively. It includes many of the themes so prevalent in Verdi's works. There is the doomed love affair, in this case, Riccardo's feelings for his friend's wife Amelia. Following on from this, there's a fatal misunderstanding on Renato's part that causes him to commit the murder. The irony is, however, that Riccardo was actually putting his feelings for Amelia aside, as he had planned to send both Amelia and Renato away together. This is another play that ends in a climax worthy of Shakespeare. Misunderstandings and jealousy resulting in the loss of life that could have been avoided. But at least there is only one death on this occasion, as opposed to the four in *Forza del Destino*...

Musically Verdi starts to move away from the pure *Bel Canto* style of Donizetti and Bellini. The characters are all given their own 'sound character', and leitmotivs are popping up throughout the opera. Wagner is definitely peeking around the corner at this point. Riccardo's main melody was the only thing Tchaikovsky was said to have liked about the opera, and it is one of its strongest musical features that brings the work together.

Rehearsing and conducting it immediately brought up the big issue of 'leading or following'. At the *Ring Cycle* rehearsals these essential matters had clearly been addressed before the stage and orchestra sessions, with Haitink being a master of balancing the two. Wagner also leaves much less room for individual freedom than Verdi does at this stage, writing a more symphonic structure. But there are still big stretches where a singer can make their own personal mark.

Whereas with concerto soloists, where it is my belief that they should always be in the driving seat, with opera it is more nuanced and complicated than that. A lot of the time, the singers are part of the overall ensemble score which needs holding together to come off at all. But at the same time, they come with their own ideas, and some of these are not always open to debate, depending on the personalities we are dealing with. I quickly learned to go in with little ambition on this front, after my early suggestion of clarifying the drama by giving some of the returning leitmotivs a different musical and emotional character each time were booed off by one half of my two Riccardos. Instead of exploring different options, there was no flexibility whatsoever. When I asked what the motivation was, the reply came through loud and clear: 'This is how I sing it.'

I also learned (almost the violent way) that when you follow some singers too much, speeds can quickly slip towards the dreary side. It seemed that one over-passionate, but under-prepared tenor was ready to punch me when I suggested that it wasn't us slowing down, but it was him, and that we were just following. I think I called it 'accommodating'...and that choice of words might well have been the igniter. Luckily, he retreated when his Amelia whispered something in his ear. Whatever she said, I am still grateful to her. These days, I make sure that forward momentum is applied at all times, and I just call it 'following' when put on the spot.

Conducting recitativo passages from this musical period is again something that deserves time and reflection before the rehearsals. I will now insist on stricter time keeping from the singers and treat it more like how it was 'composed'. If more freedom is needed, then I will work through it with them at length, so that both parties at least have a rough idea of what might unfold when suddenly the bright stage lights are on, the smoke is thick and blinding, and the tree is a wobbly one.

Crucially, what helped me was that I was there in person, playing the piano for the whole rehearsal process, and thus able to change certain habits bit by bit. For me, that 'being part of it' is not only vital in getting it done practically, but also builds team spirit, which in opera is so much more essential even than in orchestral music making.

For singers, musicians, conductors, stage directors and designers to come together as one harmonious creative force, superhuman efforts are often needed, musically, but also psychologically at times. But when they do, the resulting experience is the most rewarding one imaginable. From Monteverdi to Mozart, Verdi to Wagner, and Alban Berg to John Adams.

As the great Verdi himself said:

> *'Opera is the ultimate art form that combines the beauty of music, drama and visual aesthetics. When I am alone with my notes, my heart pounds and the tears stream from my eyes, and my emotion and joys are almost too much to bear.'*

My first steps in the real world

> *'Music is at once the product of feeling and knowledge, for it requires for its disciples, composers and performers alike, not only talent and enthusiasm, but also knowledge and perception, which are the result of protracted study and reflection.'*
> *Alban Berg*

It had become clear that there seemed to be two obvious paths into the professional conducting world. Try to get on the international competition circuit or follow the opera repetiteur route which would most likely direct me towards Germany or Austria. I wasn't keen to leave London just yet, and the Royal Opera House experience had shown that this was still an awesome and inspiring place to be. And there was the audition for the Bournemouth assistant conductorship to get through first, and Haitink had kindly agreed to advise me on the repertoire, that Brahms finale in particular.

I met him at his house a few weeks into the Wagner rehearsals, and he asked me at length if I was enjoying it and how

I thought it was all sounding. He explained that the shortage of rehearsal time was a challenge but felt that it was all coming together now. That warmth and depth of sound he was looking for was starting to seep through, and he seemed genuinely excited and relieved by that. I thought it had all been sounding out of this world from the start, but it was true that during *Die Walküre* in particular, there was a lushness to the sound that made you forget about the slightly dry theatre acoustics.

'You know, Brahms and Wagner hated each other, so this session is fun. Show me how you beat this first movement. And what about your speed choices? Six at the start or a controversial two?' I had gone for the usual broad six. But these days, I take it in a steady two, being more aware of the 'poco maestoso' which beating in two (in this case signifying 6/8), seems to create, rather than beating in 6/4. Haitink didn't seem to have a view on the choice itself, but just urged me to think about what I wanted from that opening and how it fitted into the bigger picture.

Sometimes we can tweak a tempo here and there if we think it brings the composer's message across more clearly, and a particular orchestra or venue will play a part in making that choice too. He was happy with my 'six beat'. I told him that it was the guest conductor at college who taught us to keep the inner beats low and going sideways, and to have that firm upbeat with the following downbeat preferably going down. Haitink had conducted the guest conductor in his previous guise as an orchestral player, and told stories of him being naughty at times, but he was full of respect.

We skipped to the start of the last movement and the section that worried me the most. These days I beat it all out, but then, full of youthful optimism, I didn't shy away from shifting between four and two, even one, with maybe an eight in the mix here and there. He watched me conduct for a short while, but then stopped me and kindly suggested a few tweaks. He said that they might clarify things for myself, 'which could only benefit the players', and gave me that warm smile. I tried it and of course it all made total sense.

But Haitink was still not convinced I had found the natural flow of the section, and said, 'you know, why don't I show you what I normally do. Not that I am 'right' per se, but it might give you an idea.'

Of course he was right. He picked up his own baton, took a second, then started beating, and the most amazing thing happened. The moment his stick began its flight, that sound was there, in the room. A rich and dark orchestral sound, with that silvery shine, and a sense of searching in the music. It took my breath away. There was sound without sound, just from his movements and his musical soul.

He put his stick down. Plonk. The magic was gone.

'What did you think? Was that clearer?' I was speechless but garbled something in agreement. 'Good', he said, and we then proceeded to spend a long time trying to get just a little bit of that magic into my own conducting. 'You know, you do seem to have talent, and remember, I don't have to say that. But go home and work hard, it is important. And good luck. Let me know how it went!'

Another walk home with my head in the clouds, but also a little bit wiser. And work I certainly did, maybe even too much.

I travelled to Poole by train that weekend, my brain frazzled from trying to memorise all the music and not having any idea what to expect. It was a hot day, and I'd had to get up scarily early because the conductor overseeing the auditions had summoned us hopefuls to a meeting at 9:30am, even though my audition was the last one of the day, at 4:25pm. Funnily, this man had been the teacher of my disappeared colleague at college. It is such a small world. And one I was not really part of, I felt.

There turned out to be dozens of candidates, and all of them seemed to know each other as well as the conductor-in-chief. We were ordered into the main entrance lobby, where he explained that we needed to be there a bit before our individual audition time and that we should NOT rehearse during the audition! (A very urgent instruction there, and a bit surprising given that they were looking for someone who would actively work and engage with the orchestra). We were clearly told to just beat through the section we would be asked to conduct. A long, tense pause followed, after which he looked at us meaningfully, with a faux wise smile and said, 'you know... just enjoy it.'

That was it, I had woken up at 5:30am to be told 'just to enjoy it' and not rehearse. And I now had seven hours to kill in Bournemouth, until my designated 10 minutes of enjoyment.

Apart from Brighton, which I loved, I had never had the full-on 'British Seaside Town' experience. It didn't disappoint. The centre of Bournemouth itself seemed soul-destroying to me. Derelict shops, houses in disrepair and a lot of people clearly drunk already, at midday. The beach itself was beautiful

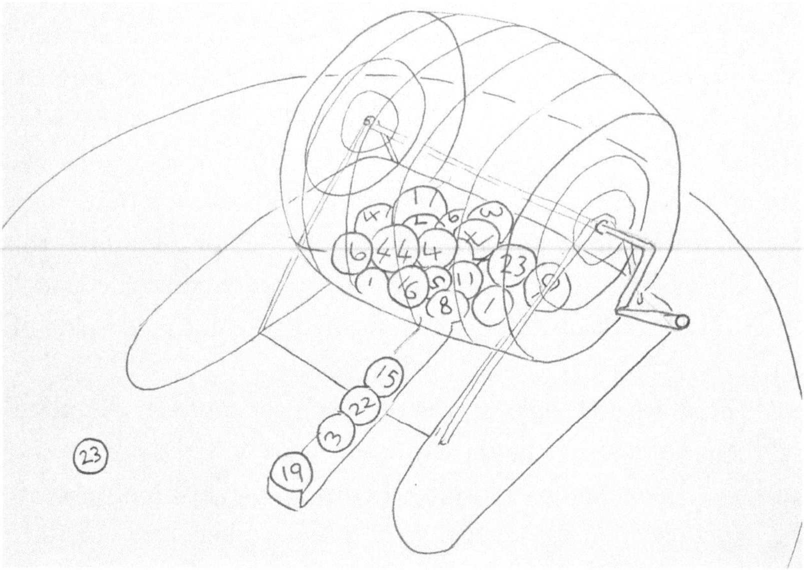

but was covered in bodies frying away like fast-food on a hotplate. I wandered around for a while, bemused and a bit dazed. Then suddenly this magical voice appeared, from afar...

'Stop and run, 81!' To my Dutch ears this was out of a fairytale, and I had no idea what was going on. 'Doctor's orders, 9!' It made no sense, yet I was drawn to the voice, and walked to where it seemed to come from. 'Dirty knee, 33!'

There was a door! I opened it quietly and tiptoed in. And there they were. What seemed like an airplane hangar full of people at the senior stages of their earthly realm, with fanatical looks in their eyes. A very jolly, very camp young man was positioned on a little stage. He was spinning the basket with the bingo balls, which looked like baby pet mice at a treadmill party and called out these bizarre phrases. 'Christmas cake, 38!' But that didn't even rhyme?! It was out of a science fiction movie to me, and weirdly claustrophobic.

I had to get out and find some peace and quiet. Which turned out to be much more difficult than I'd hoped, being stuck either on this beach or in the depressing streets of the town. So, I wandered back to the audition venue and got myself a cup of tea. It was like motor oil, superstrong with lots of cold milk, as my request for a weaker tea without milk was met with a look of disbelief and promptly ignored. And then I just sat there for many hours, trying to stop my brain going into 'remembering overdrive', and more importantly, trying to stay awake.

I woke up to a young guy prodding me, saying I was on in 10 minutes. I hastily grabbed my scores and baton and walked into the hall, where the orchestra were loudly talking and laughing, and seemingly about to leave themselves. I felt like saying, 'Get up and run, 31!' but thought better of it. Conductor-in-chief looks at me and turns to the orchestra.

'Now, just one more, ladies and gentlemen, the day is nearly done, try to stay with us just a little longer', or something along those lines. It was a novel way of introducing the last auditionee of the day. I was invited onto the rostrum and instructed to start with the Brahms.

The orchestra were still chatting, barely noticing me, let alone taking time to play. My brain was fried, making me forget some crucial queues, which frustrated me as I had spent so much time memorising it all. I have now learned that my mind needs proper downtime in between study. But what was done was done, and it seemed like no one was really taking any notice at all anyway.

Scheherazade came next, and I felt much more at home here as I had rehearsed and performed it. The orchestra were by now almost getting rowdy, like a nursery class, and not anywhere near ready to start. As conductor-in-chief was busy chatting with his fellow panel member, I decided to ask the players myself if they could please start from the suggested place in the music. This clearly was a big mistake. They briefly looked up from their conversations and proceeded to ridicule my decision to speak directly to them, loudly, and in my face. Conductor-in-chief now stands up and says, 'Ladies and gentlemen, please let's do this last little bit, and then we are free to go.' I took a deep breath, and have to say, totally nailed the *Scheherazade* sections, which meant my dignity was at least partially restored. The orchestra applauded politely, clearly instructed to do so, and I was encouraged back onto the streets of Bournemouth.

I can honestly say this was the most frustrating and dispiriting day of my time in the UK, and one that stayed with me for a long while. I bought a can of beer from the most depressing off-licence and sat down on a broken bit of curb for a time, my mind blank. Then I dragged myself up and went to the station for the long train ride home. My Wiltshire friends picked me up, and nourished my bruised ego with great food, wine and amazing family vibes.

I never heard back from the orchestra. But when I spoke to a fellow hopeful months later, he told me that they had already renewed the contract with the previous assistant who they were clearly very fond of. At least I now know that 'unlucky for some' can be lucky for someone else. And that Bournemouth in the height of summer is not for the faint-hearted.

My confidence was knocked a little, but there was no time to feel sorry for myself as I was selected to take part in the assistant conductor auditions for a Dutch orchestra, the first time they had created this position. Just a Beethoven overture, conducting two pianos. I remember walking into the auditorium, and asking the panel if they wanted me to conduct like there was an orchestra there or conduct the piano players directly. This question seemed to surprise them, and they didn't give a definitive answer. 'Just make music' was the rather cryptic reply. So, I did, and the pianists were fantastic in trying to do what I was indicating. There was lots of eye contact and a real sense of coming together musically. It lifted my spirits. There was a brief interview with the panel, which seemed positive too, but when I walked out, I overheard them saying that I had never cued the French horns.

In the end, the position went to their own principal cellist, in his early sixties, and looking for musical life after his retirement. He was a great player, great teacher and a lovely man who I remembered from the time I had accompanied one of his pupils.

I went back to London, but after these two auditions I was feeling a little less confident and certain about it all. I had done well, knew my music, went for real contact with the players, and yet it left me nowhere. But what I hated most was that the good things that were happening seemed to be overshadowed by this feeling of negativity. Some nice work was coming in with non-professional orchestras and opera societies, and that also was a great step in the right direction. I needed to build up repertoire and experience, and this was a perfect route for that. And I loved the environment, having time to share the joy of music with people who were there for that very reason.

But the self-doubt was niggling, those old candelabras, and it was threatening to take that joy away. I really needed counsel, and wondered if I would be brave enough to pick up the phone again. Haitink had said that I should feel free to contact him whenever I wanted. I had seen him conduct Mahler 4 with the LPO, so I knew he was in town.

I plucked up the courage and dialled the number. It was ringing. I looked at the clock, and saw it was half-past three. 'Do not call before 4!' suddenly went through my head. A mild panic set in. Should I put the... it was too late. His wife just answered. And with her stern voice she told me to ring back in an hour. 'You know it really needs to be after 4pm!'

When I rang again half an hour later (as the stress of waiting was just too much), he answered himself, and to my relief sounded friendly and relaxed. He would be very happy to see me and had some free time later in the week. 'Do bring some of your work!'

So, I went to his house once more, a video of me conducting various things and a bottle of classy red wine under my arm. He had refused to even discuss payment for this, so the alcohol route seemed a nice way to show my appreciation. He opened the door and immediately saw the wine. 'What is this?? That looks awfully expensive!' I said it was the least I could do, but he insisted that I shouldn't even think about something that extravagant next time. He added, though, that he was very much looking forward to sampling it that evening. And with that, I was calm and feeling like myself again, something Haitink managed to do every time I met him.

We sat down in his TV room, on the orange sofa, and after a bit of fiddling with remote controls and buttons he managed to get the video to play. I had brought Schubert's Unfinished Symphony, from one of my first concerts with the Bristol amateur orchestra for which I had recently been appointed conductor. He seemed to watch it with great interest, giving running commentary as it went along.

'I love your idea of that real quiet concentration, very good, very good. Ah, that lady finds it a bit hard', followed by warm laughter. 'You look at the whole section, not just the front desks, very good, very good' (this was a top tip from the guest conductor at college, and a crucial one). 'Woodwind a bit loud, isn't it funny, they always are.' And then he suddenly spoke with more urgency. 'Ah, now here!! More drama, much more drama!'

He said that in his teaching, he only really questioned the conductor's actions if the music didn't sound the way it should. And clearly here, it didn't. He switched off the video and said, 'Let's see if you have it in you. It might be Schubert, not Wagner, but this is incredibly dramatic and emotional music. A cry from the soul, total despair. Maybe because he knew he was most likely going to die from syphilis. We don't know, but never underplay the drama. Show me!'

So, I started beating out that section, with him humming along. He stopped me. 'Not enough, young man, we need so much more. Do it again!' It took me about 10 goes, as Haitink spurred me on, his humming getting more and more powerful. Then when I thought I'd just go totally over the top, he said 'There it is, you do have it in you! I could feel that and would have played for you! Bravo, and try to remember that feeling.'

It was like learning to listen to my own piano playing again. When we think we go too far, we probably still need several more layers. My piano teachers in Utrecht would both give me the same treatment, until I learned to properly judge my playing in terms of how it comes across to the audience. And this was the start of that in my conducting.

The hour was up, and Haitink let me out saying he would try to see me in Bristol, as his daughter lived there. But also, that he was looking into something that would be good for me to try, and that he'd be in touch. I walked home feeling like a more able conductor, and a happier man. After months of frustration, I had needed this. And it was going to get even better.

The following Monday I received an email from the Orchestral Manager of the Boston Symphony Orchestra to say that I had been scheduled-in last minute for the Summer Festival auditions at Tanglewood, on the recommendation of Bernard Haitink. I only had a week to somehow learn a whole repertoire list, book flights and get myself organised. It was total madness, and if anything, showed my lack of core repertoire. But I had to do it. An audition in Boston Symphony Hall, with a chamber orchestra made up from BSO players. It was a once in a lifetime opportunity.

I managed to get the scores together and started my crazy attempt to get all the music into my head and then into my hands. There was no time to organise lessons, Haitink was no longer in London, and I had lost touch with my teacher at college. But there were videos to watch and to 'steal, steal, steal' from.

The main piece was Debussy's *Prélude à l'après midi d'un faune*. Not a work I had conducted myself, yet I had seen it performed a lot, and every conductor seemed to be doing it differently. Which was no help whatsoever. Do I conduct the opening flute solo? Do I subdivide all the way through? And if so how, as in places the cross rhythms are so plentiful that there are many ways to tackle it. But it is a gorgeous work, dripping with sensuality. And if that can be turned into sound, then heaven reveals itself.

I decided to spend most of my precious time learning the *Prélude* and to do what I could on the other pieces. Mozart Symphony No.39 opening of movement 1, Beethoven 5 opening movement (as always), and the *Royal March* from Stravinsky's *Soldier's Tale*. That last one I had performed a few times, so it seemed in the bag at least. For the possible second round there was Tchaikovsky's Violin Concerto, with soloist. Another one I knew well but had never actually learned. To my delight (!) there would be a session of aural tests in between the two. I love them and they love me too, clearly. But, setting this one apart from the other auditions, there was also a round of feedback interviews with different orchestra members, as well as the course leader for that year, making this almost like a workshop experience, and a total win-win scenario.

I booked my flight, although the plan was nearly thwarted when I was busted for using my Mum's credit card. She had kindly offered, but try explaining that to the travel agent who thought that 'Elsa' was an unlikely first name for me (these were backward times). Luckily a quick phone call to the original Elsa resolved the situation, and we were back on track. I found a room available in a nice, centrally located hotel, and after a week of full-on note cramming, and with a brain that was screaming 'take a break!', I flew across the Atlantic for my first visit to Boston. As I would only be there for a few days, I had decided to stick to the UK time-zone, somehow trying to avoid jetlag. It meant that the audition would be at the UK equivalent of six in the evening, which was fine.

It was early spring and flying into Logan airport, the countryside seemed almost Scandinavian to me. Dark forests, silver tinted lakes and wooden farm buildings, all bathing in late afternoon sunshine. There still seemed to be a layer of ice on some of the lakes, but the weather forecasts also said it was going to be into the 20°Cs. I found the subway into town, checked into my hotel and after some questionable Chinese takeaway food, immediately crashed into a deep sleep.

My dreams were tumultuous, no doubt caused by all the excitement, and a wild car chase turned into a person screaming at me, louder and louder.

'Sir!! Sir!!' Slowly, I floated up from my jetlagged sleep, not realising immediately where I was. I could vaguely make out a young man and a trolley with champagne on it. The shine of the huge ice bucket woke me up a little more. It was probably only 9pm, but for me this was 3am in the morning, and it felt like a dream within a dream. 'Room service, Sir', he said, already with a tone suggesting he had by now realised he was in the wrong room. 'Are you Mr and Mrs Jones?' I attempted to clarify that I was not. 'Oh, I am so sorry – this is room 35'. And he and the champagne left. And I immediately sank back into my deep sleep.

Until this day, I am still not 100% sure if it wasn't a dream. But I am determined that, if there is a next time, I will be Mr and Mrs Jones! What was I thinking, sending that bottle of champagne away?!

The following day was free, and I looked forward to exploring the city. I woke up at 5am, which was novel, and had to wait two hours before breakfast was served. Time to look at scores and tire my mind out even more. Something, I now know, that is not the best way to get my mind to 'give back' when needed.

Dizzy from obsessive cramming, I went for breakfast. It didn't disappoint. Like so many things there, it was totally supersized. Waffles with maple syrup, spinach omelettes, sausages, roast beef, kippers (!!!), and more eggs of all shapes and sizes and guises. But also, hamburgers, chicken legs and some things that looked like deep-fried hamsters on a stick (corndogs they told me later). And then cakes, pastries... it just went on and on. I tried everything, apart from the impaled crispy rodents, and set out onto the streets of Boston.

The previous times I had travelled to the United States on my own had been lovely, as most people are incredibly open and sociable, even to a total stranger. Always keen to hear your story, and happy to share theirs. And I enjoyed meals on my own those times, a chance to people-watch and to really feel the atmosphere.

Boston totally blew me away. I hadn't expected it to be so historic, a leftover from my dear mother always ranting on about the lack of anything 'old' in 'that country'. Beautiful fin-de-siècle neighbourhoods, the bustling harbourside, and many lovely places to eat and drink or just sit and take it all in. I indulged in the best clam chowder and cornbread, which so far has never been rivalled.

My audition shirt urgently needed pressing and I discovered a little launderette around the corner from the hotel, where the Greek owner seemed overwhelmed by the explosive brightness of its blue colour. (This was my favourite shirt, and why blend in?) He was short man with a huge beard, dressed perfectly in suit and tie, and with a laugh that thundered through several streets. My shirt reminded him of the Aegean Sea, he said, and he was delighted to tell me his whole life story. And that of his dad, and his dad's dad, and his dad's, dad's dad. It turned out to be an adventurous romp of love, despair, adultery and ultimately hope, when the family came to Boston. And it made my afternoon. He had lots of tips for places to eat and hang out and wished me well for the auditions with a strong Greek hug. And my shirt was pressed to a standard that was unbeknownst to me up to that moment. This was why I loved my times there in the USA.

I gave myself a few more hours to revise music before another early night. Tomorrow was audition time.

Mr and Mrs Jones must have received their refreshments as planned that evening, as there were no more interruptions to my sleep. After breakfast, I was ready to go to Symphony Hall, the blue shirt as smart as it had ever looked and both of us ready to do this!

I walked there, as it was a cold but very bright and sunny morning. When I arrived and went inside the building, a strange and unexpected feeling of déjà-vu kicked in. Symphony Hall was built in 1900 and modelled on the second Gewandhaus in Leipzig, but also inspired by the Vienna Musikverein and the Amsterdam Concertgebouw. The façade is almost a brick-coloured copy of the Concertgebouw, and the foyers and lobbies are very similar too with their white walls and red plush carpets and furnishings.

It is the musical home of the world-renowned Boston Symphony Orchestra, and there were lots of photos and paintings of the illustrious conductors who had been in charge here. Serge Koussevitzky, Pierre Monteux, Charles Munch, Erich Leinsdorf, James Levine and Seiji Ozawa. There was a whole section for Bernard Haitink as their Principal Guest Conductor. He was clearly much adored here, as he was wherever he conducted. I suddenly felt a huge responsibility. I couldn't mess this up.

A group of students came out of a room together with the Course Leader of that year, one of the orchestra's guest conductors. They all seemed close and called the course leader not just by his first name, but even the informal shorter version of it (not the one I knew from CD covers). They were recalling events of the previous summer and laughing and chatting in a lively manner. I joined them at the spot where we were asked to meet, together with two fellow UK conductors. It felt a bit like the Bournemouth experience, except that everyone here was incredibly friendly and keen to share experiences, worries, audition fears and survival tactics. Most of them were indeed the Course Leader's students, and a few had been at Tanglewood before. It set the three of us from the UK apart slightly, but before we could worry about that too much, the course leader appeared and explained the order of events.

First there would be the conducting part, about 15 minutes per candidate, with time to rehearse sections if we wanted. Then the aural tests later in the afternoon, followed by the interviews the next morning, and a second round for those who got through in the evening. 'Oh, and just to make you guys more excited, Maestro Ozawa has decided to sit in on the auditions himself! Good luck, see you in there!' Starstruck, and slightly more terrified, we found our corners for some last-minute obsessing, and soon it was my turn.

The auditorium was like a temple. It was again very resemblant of the Concertgebouw, with its white panelling and chandeliers, but the stage was bigger and more set-back. It had a two-tier gallery with yet more gold and red velvet. And then there was the addition of the Greek statues, a nudge to Vienna clearly. It all felt like a cocoon of Europe here across the Atlantic. Sacred, but also warm and inviting somehow.

The orchestra were friendly. There was time for a nice handshake and a little chat with the leader, before I was asked to start. They clearly wanted us to feel as comfortable as we could. I decided to do the Debussy first, as I knew it best. But also, because I wasn't going to let a chance to conduct that astounding music, with members of the Boston Symphony and in this awesome place, be taken away from me in case of shortage of time or any other eventualities. This was about the experience, and I was going to drink it in. I stepped onto the rostrum, not wanting to create a fuss by asking to have it moved aside (which I normally do, being a very tall Dutch-legged creature).

But this rostrum was like none I had ever experienced before. It almost seemed double height, and it took quite some effort to clamber onto it. When I reached its summit, the orchestra seemed down below in the valley. There was definitely a slight, 'where are they?' moment. I had decided to keep my hands off the flute solo, and pick up conducting when the orchestra joins, something I feel most happy with still now. I had never forgotten the inviting smile, as if to say, 'please spoil us', that Jean Fournet gave to the first flute of the Concertgebouw Orchestra when he conducted it there. No instructing, just happy anticipation. And then, like everyone there, he proceeded to fall in love with the golden sound that was bestowed upon us.

The Boston flautist was a class act herself and set the tone beautifully. Luckily my brain decided to cooperate, very much because of the positive feel of these auditions. The orchestra's lush and beautiful playing in the very rich and sumptuous acoustics of the hall made it all very indulgent, and I was loving the experience of being in the middle of it. To hear phrases melt away rather than 'end' was totally wonderful.

Maybe I should have stopped and talked about the meaning of semiquavers in the viola parts or something, but I didn't want to. I was in heaven. To my amazement they let me conduct the whole thing, and luckily, the feeling of it has never left me. There was some urgent clock checking, and they asked me to do the Mozart next and rehearse it a little bit. This caught me out, as I hadn't done nearly enough work on it to be able to tell top professionals anything useful about their own playing of it. I wasn't bad, but to paraphrase Maestro Rodrigo in *Mozart in the Jungle*, I also was *not* 'not bad'.

Time was now quickly running out, and we rushed through the Stravinsky. It felt a bit like I was following their playing by now. But we finished all together, and I safely made it back to solid ground from the dizzying heights of the epic podium. There was another handshake and a genuinely warm goodbye from the players and panel, and that was it. I tried to catch a glimpse of Seiji Ozawa but could only vaguely see this little grey silhouette sitting quite far back. I figured that must have been him.

A quick sandwich and I made my way to the room where the aural tests awaited. And wow, they did not disappoint.

They were offered to us, with seeming glee, by the current Assistant Conductor. He had been in our position himself and was now clearly enjoying being on the other side. The dictation section was hilarious, making the one at the London college seem like *Mary had a little lamb*. Harmonic analysis, atonal music deciphering... it was all I had dreaded, and I was almost craving for my chair to collapse so that I could escape to go and see Redon paintings. With a certain level of embarrassment, I left the room, but enjoyed catching up with my UK compatriots who shared my sense of doom about this last hour. To forget about it all, we planned to go and see the San Francisco Symphony that evening. They were in Boston performing Copland

and Tchaikovsky and played to an incredibly high standard. Levels of precision, depth of sound and musical commitment that were second to none, easily matching the greatest European orchestras on their best days. I returned to my hotel to study the Tchaikovsky, as there was always that little chance...

My two interviews were early in the morning. First with the Course Leader, and second with the principal double bass player of the BSO. I allowed myself another gorge-fest at the breakfast buffet, still not going anywhere near the corndogs though, before heading back to the hall. I felt nervous, but I was also realistic about my chances of making it to the second round.

The Course Leader sat me down in his office. 'Ah yes, the blue shirt!' Like a medical doctor he gave me the main verdict first. He made a point of saying that I was the 'problem' candidate of that year and that they had spent a long time discussing my audition. Maybe he told every rejected candidate this, but I got the feeling he meant it. In the end they felt I was not yet ready for the festival itself, which seemed totally fair to me. But they saw talent and he laughed when he said that he could see I had taken quite a few of Haitink's conducting movements and used them to good effect. This was praise indeed, and mission accomplished there. However, he did want to share with me that Ozawa had thought my Debussy was very slow. In his eyes it became overindulgent and lacked forward momentum. I couldn't deny that I had slipped away in a cloud of 'sonic gorgeousness', and that forward momentum had not been on my mind. The note was taken though, and I vowed I would not allow it to happen again.

The second interview, with the principal double bass, was much longer, and a revelation. My blue shirt was mentioned again, as was the panel's long discussion about me. So, it really was genuine! I hadn't let Haitink down, which was very important to me. And what then followed was really like a workshop. A good half an hour of being able to talk about the things that he, as a principal orchestral player (but also a talented conductor and teacher himself), had noticed, and things I could improve upon.

'Make sure everybody sees your beat all the time, even when 'addressing' a specific section.' I remember a secret giggle when he said that not everybody might agree with Maestro Ozawa's interpretations, but that everyone did agree that he was a master of 'being seen'.

'Stay ahead of the orchestra mentally and try not to have too much physical distance from the orchestra', something he had felt was the case in the Mozart. He then looked at me and said, 'God, how tall even are you?' It got us talking about the different positions a conductor can take when in front of an orchestra, and that without a higher-sized rostrum, Maestro Ozawa would not be seen at all. I jokingly recalled being a bit dizzy all the way on top of that rostrum and having to almost locate the orchestra. He laughed and said that, if there was a next time, it would be perfectly acceptable to ask for it to be moved to the side. But the Bournemouth experience had scarred me a bit and I would not have dared to do so. And it would have made little difference. There was another warm handshake, and his genuine wish for me to try again the following year.

This had been the most positive experience I could have hoped for and totally the opposite of the previous ones. I had done well and learned so much. I realised that I seriously needed to build repertoire, keep musical momentum, and urgently brush up on my theory. 'Get to work, it is important', as Haitink had said. But I seemed to have been a serious consideration for one of the greatest festivals in the world, or at least a second-round audition of it, in a field of the most talented conductors out there. My self-confidence was restored. I now had a clear goal, and an even clearer idea of how to get there.

I went to the airport and bought a blue Father Christmas snowdome in the giftshop sale for 89 cents. It had been sitting lonely on the shelf for nearly three months. After quite a search, I finally found a rare, and now near extinct, phone box and called my Mum to tell her I was about to fly back. 'Don't relax too much', she replied, 'as something quite exciting has developed for you here, whilst you were in Boston, I will tell you later.'

And it sure had, but it very much deserves its own chapter.

Post-script

Months later, a good friend sent me a newspaper review of a concert given by the Vienna Philharmonic at the Concertgebouw in Amsterdam with Seiji Ozawa conducting. 'I thought you might enjoy this, and it will make you feel better about yourself!'

The review raved about the sound the orchestra had made, as well as Ozawa's revelatory interpretation of Dvořák's Seventh

Symphony. But they felt the opening piece, Debussy's *Prélude à l'après midi d'un faune*, was much too slow, drowning the work with its own lushness in the process.

I had to laugh and couldn't help but feel smug.

Prélude à l'après midi d'un faune

'Music is the arithmetic of sounds as optics is the geometry of light.'

'People don't very much like things that are beautiful...they are so far from their nasty little minds.'

'A beautiful sunset that was mistaken for a dawn.'

'Listen to no-one's advice except that of the wind in the trees. That can recount the whole history of mankind...'

'How much has to be explored and discarded before reaching the naked flesh of feeling?'

'There is nothing more musical than a sunset. He who feels what he sees will find no more beautiful example of development in all that book which, alas, musicians read but too little: the Book of Nature.'

'Music is the space between the notes.'

'But music, don't you know, is a dream from which the veils have been lifted. It's not even the expression of a feeling. It's the feeling itself.'

'There's never one sunrise the same or one sunset the same.'

'Art is of absolutely no use to the masses.'

'Proust is long-winded, precious, and a bit of an old woman.'

'There is no theory. You merely have to listen. Pleasure is the law.'

When we think of Claude Debussy, we immediately place him at the forefront of the Impressionist music movement, together with Maurice Ravel and composers like Francis Poulenc and Ernest Chausson. But ironically, that term, 'Impressionism', had originally only been used as a sarcastic comment by an art critic who had viewed an exhibition of Claude Monet's paintings and deemed them just 'vague impressions, nothing more than sketches at best.' And it was a name strongly rejected by the artists and musicians of the day. They preferred to regard themselves as true realists, showing the world in all its momentary and passing glory.

Similarly, Debussy argued that his music was realism. And it wasn't the works of Monet and Seurat he loved, but the pre-Raphaelite paintings, and Whistler and Hokusai. But of course, that almost super-realism, which aimed not just to convey the actual image, or strict musical form or melody, but also the emotion that comes with (or from) it, was achieved by starting to blur the edges. And with that, heightening the presence of atmosphere and feeling that we only experience perhaps unconsciously.

As we learn from his own comments, Debussy had always been looking for ways to break free from the strict rules of classical music, both harmonically and form-wise. His music teacher had described him as being very talented at harmony, but desperately careless. Camille Saint-Saëns went several steps further in a letter to his colleagues at the Paris Conservatoire: 'I advise you to look at the two pieces Mr. Debussy has just published. We must at all costs bar the door of the institute against a man capable of such atrocities!'

And it seems that in Debussy's earlier life, discipline was also missing a lot of the time. Often referred to as 'an egotist', he was nearly always in debt and experienced several failed romantic relationships.

'That Debussy is nothing but a pleasure seeker', according to composer and conductor Paul Vidal, who won the Prix de Rome the year before Debussy did. It didn't stop them from becoming friends though, and they famously performed Liszt's *Faust* Symphony in Rome on two pianos in 1886, with Liszt allegedly sleeping through the whole performance. But Claude Debussy was starting to come of age as a person and as a composer, with his journey of development funded for a great part by his close friend, Ernest Chausson.

Around 1887, the 25-year-old Debussy began attending the Tuesday evening soirées at the apartment of the Symbolist poet Stéphane Mallarmé. Regular guests included the sculptor Rodin, the painter Claude Monet, the poets Paul Verlaine and Paul Valéry, and writers like Marcel Proust. The connections and real friendships he made there turned out to have a lasting influence on his music. And bit by bit, he was being noticed and even appreciated by the establishment in Paris.

It was then, after his song cycle *Fêtes Galantes* and his cantata *La Damoiselle élue* had been accepted by the very snooty Société Nationale de Musique, that he started working on the piece that, in the words of Pierre Boulez, 'made the art of music begin to beat with a new pulse.'

The *Prélude à l'après-midi d'un faune*, based on the poem of the same name by Mallarmé, took shape between 1892 and 1894, when Debussy was also working on his string quartet. The *Prélude* turned out to be a masterpiece unlike anything heard before, and with which he finally found the liberation from rules that he had been so passionate about. He describes his

Prélude as 'a very free illustration of Mallarmé's poem… to evoke the successive scenes in which the longings and desires of the faun pass in the heat of the afternoon.'

Debussy, who knew Mallarmé quite well by 1892, might initially have thought about writing incidental music to an acted-out performance of the poem. When he played the *Prélude* to Mallarmé on the piano, in his apartment, the poet was dumbfounded, exclaiming 'I didn't expect anything like this! This music prolongs the emotion of my poem and sets its scene more vividly than colour.'

Originally, the work was planned to have three movements: a Prelude, followed by an Interlude and then a *Paraphrase Finale*. However, when making his final revisions of the *Prélude*, Debussy discarded the sketches for the last two movements, and on 22 December 1894, the audience of the Société Nationale heard the premiere of a single-movement symphonic poem. And like 'impressionist' painting, Debussy dealt deliberately in vagueness; his music suggesting rather than depicting. With its unusual combinations of tonal colour, the *Prélude* is a study of light and shadow. Its general form is clear, but the design is characteristically non-symphonic, with hazy outlines.

The story of Stéphane Mallarmé's poem centres around a mythological faun who is half man, half goat. The faun is playing his flute and falls asleep. He dreams sensuously of two nymphs, but when he wakes up, reality is the same as before. He then tries to re-live the dream in his mind:

> *I would perpetuate those nymphs.*
> *Their rosy bloom's so light, it floats upon air drowsy with sleep.*

That first performance might have had the critics divided in their response, but the audience adored it: the whole piece was encored, and a repeat performance of the entire programme was given the following day, with the Société opening its doors to the general public for the first time.

Debussy's orchestration for the *Prélude* is not especially large: no trumpets or trombones and no timpani. But the wind section receives extra sonority through the addition of a third flute and a Cor Anglais.

These days, we respond to the iconic opening with a feeling of comfortable familiarity. But at the time, the uniquely created instrumental shadings came across as if the orchestra was a newly restored painting. Following the 'lonely' flute melody, Debussy creates a dreamlike atmosphere through avoiding clear-cut harmonies, to which his colours of rustling strings, cascading woodwinds, passionate outbursts from the full orchestra, and, near the magical close, those ethereal antique cymbals, prove themselves ideally suited.

Its freedom and vagueness bring a whole spectrum of conducting issues, that very flute solo being the first one we have to consider. As so often, there is the choice whether to lead or to follow, just like in opera. Having discussed this with many flautists, there doesn't really seem to be a preference, so perhaps that decision is best made, at least mostly, based on their wishes.

Then there is an episode towards the end of the *Prélude*, when the main melody returns, but now played by the full or-

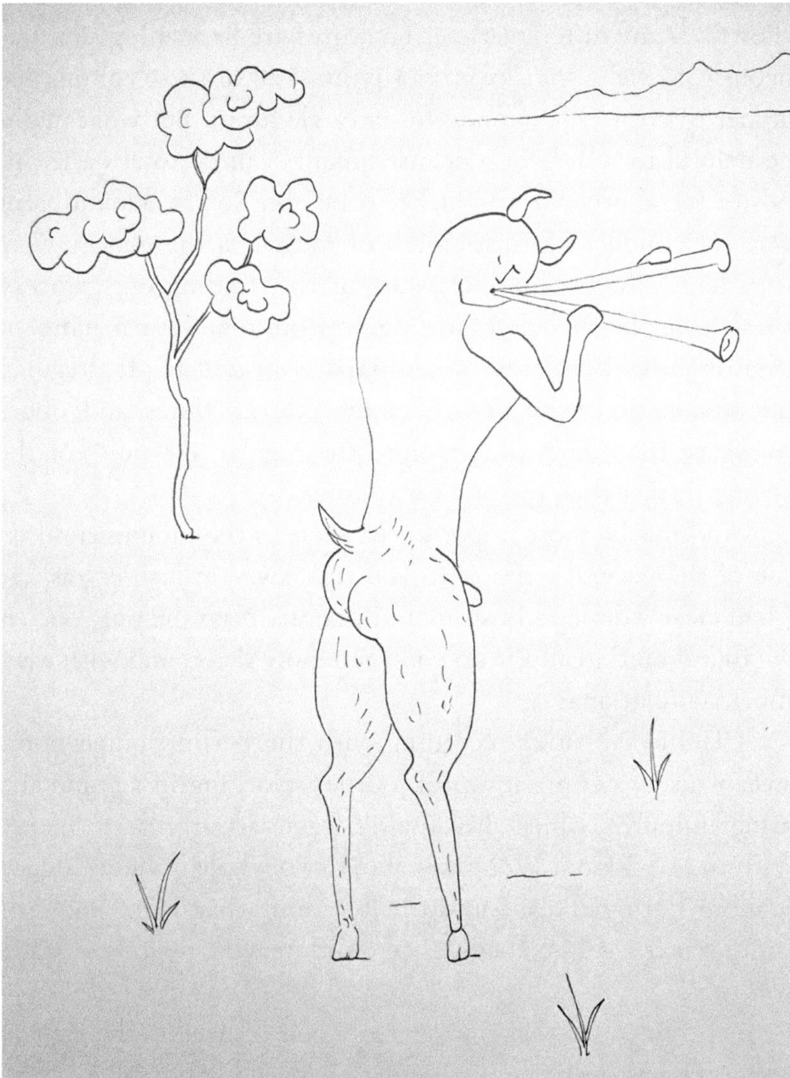

chestra. Many different time signatures are happening simultaneously, as well as tricky cross rhythms, all of these coming together to create that wonderful fairytale forest. But what might be helpful for one group of instruments can be totally the opposite for another. I was lucky to be able to try out different ways of conducting this stretch of music, as the players were very happy to be an active part of the 'finding out' process. I now beat the six bars following on from that 'return' moment (figure 10 in the score, for the purists) in non-triplet 'regular' quavers, as it seemed much easier for the flutes and oboes to weave their 12/8 time around the regular 4/4 pulse of the strings, rather than the other way around.

And maybe most importantly, there is the monumental issue of the general tempo. Do you sink away in lush ecstasy, as I had clearly done in Boston (and I hadn't been the only one, as we found out later)? Or do you keep more drive, and with that, more acute drama?

Claudio Abbado's recording with the Berlin Philharmonic sweeps us away on a mystical journey, clocking in at nine and a half minutes, whilst Stokowski's legendary live performance with the LSO from 1972 takes about two whole minutes longer. I adore both but can now finally admit that I am addicted to that extra bit of sensuality. And maybe secretly, Ozawa was too...

It is fair to say that the original poem, as well as the *Prélude*, plays not just with the distinctions between dream and reality, but also with creative vision and desire. It is probably no surprise that the much more literal staging by Diaghilev's Ballet Russes, with Vaslav Nijinsky as the Faun, scandalized audiences in 1912, when it seemingly crossed the line between artistic allusion and sexual fantasy.

'The *Prélude* opened a whole new world to music', Igor Stravinsky noted. He later also wrote that Debussy was his greatest musical influence, and after the masterpieces that followed the *Prélude; La Mer* (based on Hokusai's wave), his opera *Pelléas et Mélisande* and ballet *Jeux*, written for the Ballet Russes, Debussy's place at the very top of the French musical establishment had been truly cemented.

He even made it onto the exam board of the Paris Conservatoire, probably much to Saint-Saëns' wrath. And Debussy clearly never lost his sarcastic sense of humour, famously stating after one set of exams that, 'The jury had included some very odd musicians who would have been more at home judging livestock'. And that he hoped to be able to survive twelve student performances of his own Clarinet Rhapsody.

Claude Achille Debussy died in March 1918, the fearful and dark last two years of his life being the opposite of the colourful magic of his music. Even though he had finally found happiness with Emma Bardac and their little daughter Chou Chou, Paris was being battered by German bombs and he was terminally ill with cancer, writing to a friend that music had totally abandoned him. The Violin Sonata, written in 1917, had been his autumnal farewell to the world, yet still a piece full of vibrant rhythms, shimmering colours and warm nostalgia.

His death at a time when Paris was close to being obliterated by bombing was only noticed by a small section of the classical music world that was still active at that time, as the war was still raging. Chou Chou, twelve years old and heartbroken, wrote to her half-brother. 'Papa is dead, those three words... I don't understand them, or maybe I understand them too well.' In his life, he had indeed made music beat with a new pulse.

> *'There is no theory. You have only to listen. Pleasure is the law. I love music passionately. And because I love it, I try to free it from barren traditions that stifle it. It is a free art gushing forth – an open-air art, boundless as the elements, the wind, the sky, the sea. It must never be shut in and become an academic art.'*
> *Claude Debussy*

To the Land of Vampires

> *'Conductors make too much fuss of conductors. Humility and hard work are virtues. We are nothing without our musicians.'*
> *Sir Simon Rattle*

'Make sure to take dollars with you!', my Stepdad had been saying for weeks. It seemed silly to me, as we were in modern times, and surely dollars were the last thing that would be accepted in a country like Romania. 'You never know, they might be helpful in an unexpected situation, just take them!' Even though it sounded like the advice of someone stuck in the Cold War, I gave in, if anything to stop the constant nagging about it. A hundred dollars in small notes, hidden away with my travel papers. Meanwhile, my dear Oma had been having nightmares about me going missing and her searching the country, in a taxi driven through snow-covered forests, for weeks on end. Clearly everyone was very optimistic about my first proper professional engagement.

Whilst I was in Boston, a cunning plot had come together in which my conducting abilities were traded for a Dutch tour by the Transylvanian String Quartet, made up of principal players from the State Philharmonic Orchestra in Cluj. It was rapidly becoming clear that the world of musical opportunities was often an exchange market. The orchestra went for it, providing I could bring with me a substantial new repertoire piece for them. Of course, I grabbed this chance with both hands.

The plans came together quickly, and we decided on the overture: *Cyrano de Bergerac* by the late romantic Dutch composer Johan Wagenaar. Together with Max Bruch's famous First Violin Concerto and Dvořák's Eighth Symphony, we created what we thought would be a popular programme, perfect as a warmup for the orchestra's annual autumn festival the following week. The Dutch Embassy in Bucharest was very enthusiastic about supporting this exchange of cultural heritage and had agreed to enable the project financially. The music was ordered and sent directly to Romania, and I made all the arrangements for the journey at my parents' local travel agents.

My hometown of Doorn, which is situated on the mildly undulating Utrechtse Heuvelrug (or 'Hill-Ridge', its lack of any actual hills being the butt of jokes for many non-Dutch visitors), has hardly any international credentials. Apart from, that is, being the place where the last German Emperor ended up after the First World War. And from where he refused to leave ever again, dead or alive. His tomb is still there, much to the chagrin of consecutive German governments who wanted him back to complete the line-up of Emperors in the Berlin Palace after the reunification in 1990. So far, they have had no luck.

It is delightfully provincial, but close to Utrecht and Amsterdam, so international travel document requirements would certainly be common knowledge for the local travel industry, you would think. Flying to Budapest was by far the easiest option, they told me, as that way no visa was required, and then I could take a train from there to Cluj. The orchestra were putting me up in a glamorous looking 'old-world' hotel in the city's central square. It all looked straightforward enough.

I had been able to rehearse and perform the programme in Bristol the term before, which was a luxury, and I had come to really like the Wagenaar overture. You couldn't help but think that a score of Richard Strauss' *Don Juan* had never been far away from Wagenaar's desk, but the work has a lot of merit of its own and made me discover more of his compositions, which are rarely played even in the Netherlands. (I remember Haitink complaining that Holland always preferred non-Dutch to Dutch, from musicians to compositions and even football players, and I think he certainly had a point).

My bags were packed, the dollars stashed away in a side pocket, and my parents dropped me off at Schiphol airport. My closest friend and I would always aim to meet at the Dakota Café there before setting off on our various travels. Together we had survived the DOJO youth orchestra, fascinating parental adventures and the onslaught that was music college, and this spot was the perfect symbol of stepping away from routine and life's challenges. Drinking beer and eating *Bitterballen* served by Carla, who had seen it all and seemed to possess uncanny psychic powers, whilst watching the planes depart to their destinations in the big, wide world. Everything would make sense again. My friend wasn't here this time, but Carla was, so I went up and had a quick drink for good luck. This was the biggest adventure in my professional life so far, and I had no clue what to expect.

The short flight arrived on schedule in Budapest, which meant that I had good time to make my way to one of the three main railway stations for the connecting train to Cluj-Napoca. The taxi ride was uneventful, which I thought was a good sign, and I got there with time to spare. The station building was beautiful and looked like it had been stolen from central Paris. The red, fluorescent sign of a huge McDonald's next to it spoilt the dream a little, but also showed how the western commercial brands were starting to become part of life here.

I looked up at the departure boards but couldn't see a destination even vaguely resembling the name Cluj, or any train leaving at the time mine was supposed to. There were many helpdesks, so I took a deep breath and walked up to the nearest one. I thought it would be best to speak German, but the bemused looking lady shut her window very abruptly after my short attempt to explain the situation. Taken aback, I tried the neighbouring desk, and the same thing happened. By now, my heart rate was up considerably, and, as I usually do without realising it, I had started to rattle through my available options out loud. Together with causing many bemused looks from the people in the station, it luckily also alerted a French gentleman who kindly pointed me towards the far end of the hall, where I could just about make out a small, dark window with 'International' written above it.

I knocked on the glass and an elderly lady slowly, and only partially, opened the window. 'Ja, bitte?' she said, in a gravelly voice that suggested a lifelong passion for whisky and cigarettes. German it was. She grabbed my ticket, took ages to inspect it, and then shook her head. I found out there and then that Cluj is not called Cluj in Hungarian. But much more crucially, that my train to 'Klausenburg', or 'Kolozsvár', didn't leave from this station at all, but from the one on the other side of the city. And in 15 minutes. She was delighted to tell me that the following train did go from here, and in 'only' five hours from now! I thanked her profusely and once again considered my choices, not that there really were any. The later train would still get me into Cluj at a reasonable time, and my ticket allowed me to travel on it. Racing to the other side of the city in a quarter of an hour was not realistically possible. I phoned home via reverse charge call (something that was to become a feature of this trip, much to my in-laws' wrath) and asked my parents to contact the agent so she could let the orchestra know to expect me in the evening rather than the afternoon.

My good intentions to immerse myself in the local culture went straight out of the window, as all I craved were those red neon signs and a Big Mac, bringing a vague feeling of home and the familiar. For the next four hours, McDonald's was my haven of escapism, trying to memorise more of the Wagenaar whilst gorging on fast-food.

When I got back to the station, the big black boards did show Kolozsvár this time. The train itself seemed a museum piece, from barely beyond the steam era. I climbed onto the little wobbly steps, and we left as planned in the middle of the afternoon, the roughly 400km taking a whopping eight hours. I installed myself in a compartment filled with a group of friendly German medical students, who were going to Romania to study the effects of outdated X-ray equipment on the human body, trying to see if there was a link with high cancer rates. It hit home that my destination was by then still only starting to catch up with the rest of the western world.

My new travel companions were very sociable, and we had been talking enthusiastically about life and what to expect in Cluj. I was surprised that they said they had to buy a visa, as I had been clearly told by the travel agents that it was fine to travel without one. Probably a German requirement, I thought to myself, and brushed the doubts out of my mind.

We reached the Romanian border after only a couple of hours. The train came to a shuddering halt, and a large group of army personnel entered. They looked like they were still in their teenage years and were carrying large rifles.

'Visa!!' was the loud and very clear message. My panic was right back. Oma's dream suddenly became a reality in my mind. Her in that taxi, and I imprisoned in a snowy, far away part of this country.

An older, more senior-ranking man walked up to me and asked if there was a problem. His German was fluent, so at least I could explain my unfortunate predicament. The Customs Officer checked my passport and travel papers and went to his sidekick to discuss things. He looked at me suspiciously and said 'Haben Sie dollars? Für dollars können wir ihnen ein vorübergehenden visum verkaufen.' I couldn't believe what I was hearing. My Stepdad was forgiven in a flash, as relief gushed through my system. 'I do, I do', I said, and showed him the secret stash. 'Dann ist alles in Ordnung.' He produced a form, which he signed and handed over. 'That will be fifteen dollars, nur in cash.'

My German friends had been silent this whole time, but now looked up in great surprise. I handed over a twenty dollar note, asking if they had change. 'Nur in Romanian Leu', and he proceeded to open a large suitcase which was stuffed full of banknotes. He took what looked like two random handfuls and scrunched them into mine. 'Danke, und eine gute Reise.'

I was in a daze and struggled to get the mountain of green paper into my wallet. The officers then spent what seemed like an age turning seats over, seemingly looking for possible stowaways, before allowing the train through. It had been more than an hour. Michael, one of the medics, leaned over. 'Are you alright?' he asked. And then slightly pissed off, 'Do you know that we had to pay over one hundred Deutschmarks per visum for ours?' Next time they would know: listen to your Stepdad, book the trip at a small-town travel agent and take dollars with you. Even if it brings a slight risk of a heart attack, or family search parties in the snow.

The Romanian leg of the journey went at a very leisurely pace to put it mildly. No faster than what seemed like 15 miles per hour, and occasionally stopping at tiny platforms in the middle of nowhere, with often just a single person joining or leaving the train. They might as well just have jumped on and off with the speed at which we were travelling. Maybe some people had. The countryside was lush, and it all felt like we had stepped back in time. Farmers in traditional outfits using horse drawn equipment, animals roaming over the tracks freely and many small wooden houses, often in a serious state of disrepair. We were in Transylvania now, the land of Count Vlad Dracul.

'His castle sitting on the very edge of a terrific praecipe...Chasms with silver threads where rivers wind in deep gorges and forests', as Bram Stoker described in his famous novel. It was easy to picture it and to imagine those tales of the Count's evil pursuits. After many hours, nature just seemed to vanish, to be replaced by grey concrete housing blocks. We were in the outskirts of Cluj. We gently rolled into the central train station, which looked strangely like the Rijksmuseum in Amsterdam in its design. It was 9pm in the evening, and I just wanted a bath and a bed. And wine. Not in any specific order.

A very smiley gentleman was waiting for me on the platform. He had a huge and very pink poster that had my name on it, advertising the concert. Seeing it, bright and colourful, lifted my spirits immediately. Thankfully the message of my delay had gotten through and it was the right location this time. I hugged my German compatriots, arranged to have coffee during the week, and set off with my new host. He spoke immaculate English and showed me the sights of the city as we drove to the hotel. Once again, Paris came to mind when taking in the architecture, but it was somehow in a Bohemian style.

Cluj is the second most populated city in Romania, and the unofficial capital of Transylvania. Culturally and academically, it is seen as the country's foremost centre, and the astounding buildings suggested great riches when it had been part of Hungary. The hotel was located on Unirri Square, just opposite St Michael's church, and looked properly regal. It took you right back to the late nineteenth century, with Prussian and Bohemian royalty staying there for decadent times, wining, dining and partying. By now, the glamour had faded, and the hotel looked tired. But that regality was still there, even if it urgently needed a face-lift.

I decided to skip dinner and go straight to bed, as the first rehearsal was the very next morning. I was going to meet with the Orchestral Manager and Leader a few hours before, so that we could introduce ourselves and go through plans for the week ahead. I waved my host goodbye, ordered a glass but received what turned out to be the first of many bottles of Riesling that week, and collapsed in my room. This was home for the next five days and it had a bath! (If no plug, but we could deal with that later). Things were looking up. Surely after today, it could only get less eventful.

The rehearsals took place in the main university hall where the concert would be performed. The Orchestral Manager and Leader were both very welcoming and friendly. They really appreciated that I had created a rehearsal schedule in advance, keeping the necessity of attendance for the different sections in mind, something that clearly didn't happen often. The only problem was that the music for the overture hadn't arrived yet. This surprised me, as it had been sent many weeks ago, and should be trackable. But this was Romania in 1997, and the general feeling was that it would probably have been held at the border somewhere. We decided to hope for the best, start with the Dvořák today, and if the overture was not there by tomorrow, we would pick another piece to open the concert.

The orchestra were all in their seats, and my first ever fully professional rehearsal was about to start. There was applause as a welcome, and some Romanian words for me to learn. I looked up, and to my surprise, the brass section was positioned in the middle of the orchestra behind the strings, where the woodwind would normally be. And the woodwind was on either side, where you would normally expect the brass to be.

As my brain was still slightly misty from the day before, I genuinely thought this might be the Romanian way of doing things. So, I innocently asked if, for this particular concert, they wouldn't mind setting up 'UK-style', joking that over there, everything was done the other way around. Cars drive on the wrong side of the road, and they pour cold milk into weak coffee. And brew their tea into motor oil. The players laughed at this, and whispered things in an approving way. To more applause the woodwind quickly moved to the middle, and the brass moved to the sides. Spotting that there was no doubt over how the players would position themselves in this set up, I realised that it must have been a practical 'new young conductor' joke. And by missing that, I had done exactly the right thing!

The Leader then asked if I would prefer to rehearse in Romanian or French, as they were the only languages that the players were familiar with. English didn't seem to be an option. My French was rusty but not too bad, so we agreed that would be the way forward. I took a deep breath, and we dove into that glorious opening melody of Dvořák's most folk-inspired symphony.

A first rehearsal is in many ways my favourite. Just playing through the pieces, conductor and orchestra getting a feel for each other, and being able to find out what would come together naturally, and what would need unpicking. I realised quickly that the timpani player liked to make his presence known, the higher end of the dynamic scale being where he preferred to operate. The strings had this sound that seemed of a bygone era. It reminded me of a Bruno Walter recording. Somehow cleaner than nowadays, more *portamenti* built in, and incredibly free in the flow. I did notice that it took time for the players to pick up speeds. I felt they were following each other more than immediately taking on my tempi. This told me to really be ahead mentally, just as the Boston Symphony bass player had told me.

We ran the symphony and worked on the first movement in some more detail. My college teacher had said that it was a good thing, early in a rehearsal period, to take one tricky section and really dissect it, as if to say, 'we are taking this seriously'. But that first day didn't seem the best time to do this, so I kept it relaxed and all about musically finding each other. And it allowed me to get used to conversing in French as well. Step by step. *Pas à pas!*

We finished a bit early, which went down well with everyone, and I walked back to the office to see if the Wagenaar had arrived. Sadly, it hadn't. They said they had phoned the publisher, who seemed puzzled by it all, and who would deal with them directly. But for now, we had to think of another overture we could do, as there were only four days left. This wouldn't be enough time to get *Cyrano* to a proper standard, even if the music did arrive. It was a big symphonic poem.

Together with the Leader, I went into the music library and agreed that Mozart's *Figaro* Overture would be a good choice. It kept the concert light and not too long, which was perfect. We all knew it well, and I thought it would be ideal for getting in a few historically informed touches, as I was starting to really enjoy that aspect of performing and rehearsing the classical repertoire.

The afternoon was all mine to explore the city, after first finding some lunch somewhere. I opted for a salad bar-type place, as I was a bit intimidated by the language barrier and the very stern sounding people on the streets. They really were quite aggressive verbally and looked angry most of the time. The squares and buildings were very impressive, and I found a lovely park where many young couples seemed to come to enjoy each other's company and to show their affection. A big fountain in the middle made it feel very Italian. Under the big plane trees and in the warm autumn sun I just sat, trying to make sense of it all, and promptly fell asleep.

After nearly an hour, I wandered back to the hotel to start marking up the Mozart and to make notes for tomorrow's rehearsal. Suddenly we had a lot of extra time, with the *Figaro* being only five minutes long, and I had to think what best to do. Be brave and suggest earlier finishing times, or rehearse for longer? I opted for the latter, as I could always change that if it felt we were getting bored. The main challenge now was dinner, and I decided to eat in the hotel restaurant this first night. The menu looked good, and the prices were all incredibly low when calculated in UK currency. Or dollars, if it all went horribly awry.

The dining room was magnificent. It must have been the original ballroom, with a shining parquet floor, mirror walls and ornate panelling, high ceilings with much gold, and huge crystal chandeliers.

When I walked in, the team of young waiters clocked me and started talking to each other quietly. One of them came up, welcomed me in good English and showed me where I could sit. There were about 50 tables, but only four of them had diners. In the corner, a little band of folk musicians was playing. The lead violinist was a lot older than his two colleagues but clearly a properly trained and very virtuoso player. Accompanied by double bass and keyboard, the music was what we would describe as 'gypsy' music, mostly improvised, but with the odd classic thrown in. Monti's *Czardas* unfolded as I had never heard it before, but probably as it had been intended.

The same waiter took my food order, and I asked for a glass of the Riesling. And like the night before, a bottle appeared. I suggested that I really did just want a glass, but the waiter looked at me apologetically, suggesting that his English wasn't good enough to understand what I was on about. I could only oblige and have a good attempt at finishing it. This very much became the ritual of my dining experiences that week.

At the end of the meal, the band stopped playing, and the leader turned to us diners. His face was angry, and he uttered many loud words with his bow swinging wildly in the air. My Romanian was not up to scratch, but he was clearly swearing. I went over to hand them a tip, as it seemed our stinginess was what had set him off. This luckily pacified his temper and got us chatting.

All three of them spoke very good English, which was a relief. He himself used to play in the Philharmonic and was impressed I was there as the guest conductor for that week. His colleagues had travelled all over Europe, and to our amazement it turned out that the keyboard player was a good friend of a violinist I used to know at music college in Utrecht. The same violinist who used to climb onto the college roof and practise there for hours each day. There were endless complaints from neighbours, but he persevered and was a student celebrity for that very reason. This was the final ice breaker, and the band joined me at my table, helping me polish off the remaining Riesling. It was soon time for bed, and I would see them again the next evening. I signed for the bill and went back to my room, managed to seal the bath's plug-less plughole with a cleverly manipulated plastic bag and an ashtray, and after a long soak I drifted off into a deep sleep.

The next morning, I walked into the rehearsal hall and was able to greet everyone in Romanian, as taught to me by the hotel band. 'Buna Dimineata!'

The Wagenaar was still illusive, so I introduced the Mozart to the orchestra, a choice that seemed to go down well. The first run through was easy. They played it well, be it in their own broad speed and with a rich, Brahms-like sheen. I should probably have run with that, but I thought this piece would give me a good chance to go into more detail about style. That way, I wouldn't be seen to be criticising anyone, but would still make it clear that we were here to work hard and to get the best result.

We started again, and I stopped after the first seven bars or so, trying to explain the phrasing, the dynamic detail, the vibrato, the length of last notes...All this in second-rate French, and clearly sounding like I knew it all and that they had just produced total nonsense. The players looked at me like they had literally just woken up from a long nap. We played it again. It sounded exactly the same as the first time around. So, I stopped and politely asked if we could pay more attention this time. Suddenly there was mumbling. I got a little irritated, which must have been apparent in my voice, as the players now stared at me with a sense of bewilderment, like they'd spotted a person screaming loudly at a tree in a forest or something. The Leader leant over to me and whispered in my ear. 'It is not your ideas, do not worry, but for now, best to just move on, and maybe add little touches in the coming time. It is still early days.' He gave me a wink, and we played through the piece one last time, before swiftly moving on to the Dvořák.

A big lesson was learnt at that very moment. Go with what the orchestra gives you and find merit in that. And then adapt little things, *pas à pas*. Or in Cluj, 'pas cu pas', especially when you are on your first engagement! Haitink had explained it so well, and I chose to forget it there and then. But it did help me a lot in the rest of that rehearsal, as we had a good session on the middle movements of the symphony. I listened properly and didn't throw preconceived ideas at them for the sake of it. What a wonderful way to work, when it becomes an exchange. And it felt like it was starting to be just that.

The clarinets made my day with how they melted away their crucial phrase in the second movement. I asked them do it again, just out of greed, and the orchestra applauded. A corner seemed to have been turned.

Much relieved, I finished the rehearsal a bit early again. I had to rush to the travel agents, to organise my seat reservations for the journey home at the weekend. The gentleman spoke decent German but seemed in a constant state of anger and annoyance with me. I had experienced a lot of that over the last few days. When I tried to enquire politely about something, I was either ignored or bashed out of the way by other people. And when someone did eventually speak to me, it was with exasperation.

'No, no, no! You must take the bus, it is cheaper!' the man snapped at me. 'Well yes, but I have already booked the train, and I just need the seats', I replied. 'The train really is a waste of money; I will find you bus tickets!' he insisted. 'That is very kind, but I have the train tickets here, look!! I just need seats.' 'You see, this is the bus timetable, and it saves you...'

At this point, I realised there was no hope, so I thanked him for his time and walked out. I bumped into a young lady on the pavement, who quietly, but with real bite, said that she could get me a lot of Romanian Leus if I had any dollars. I thanked her as well and ran back to the peace and quiet of my hotel room

Lunch had been a quick slice of Cluj-style pizza. A crazy number of tasteless black olives and something that seemed to be cheese and ham all rolled into one, pink and gloopy. I was starving, and looked forward to dinner in the glorious ballroom, sharing today's adventures and remains of the mandatory bottle of Riesling with my new band friends. On cue, not mine but the waiter's, the bottle was plonked on my table with the menu, and I ordered. The musicians waved at me, and everything seemed set for a calm night. I was fantasising about having another long bath.

On the table next to me sat a large middle-aged gentleman in full military regalia. He was covered with lots of medals and wore impressively shiny leather boots. 'Maybe a General?' I remember thinking. With him, also dressed up, were two elderly ladies (his aunts, perhaps) and a couple of younger men. It seemed a happy family occasion, involving lots of champagne. Like every night, I divided my time between eating, drinking the Riesling and listening to the music, but I had seen the waiter being called to the festive table and the General whispering something in his ear. Waiter disappears and returns with another big bottle of champagne, which he brings to my table. 'With highest compliments from the General', he said. My first thought was that I had been right, he really was a General! My second was one of utter surprise. 'Is he a fan of Wagenaar? Does he think I am someone I am not?'

I must have looked a bit freaked out, as at this point the musicians stop playing and join me at my table. They ask about my day, but swiftly the conversation moves on to the bottle of Dom Perignon in front of us. I tell them it was a gift from the other table, which prompts a bigger reaction than I had expected.

The lead violinist gets up to chat to the waiter, quietly, in a corner of the room, and returns with a look of worry on his face. He moves close to me and says, in a hushed voice, 'I have the dubious honour of telling you that the General has decided he would like to have you as his birthday present tonight.'

It took a bit of time for that message to sink in, before, like a bombshell, a sense of utter disbelief came over me. I guess as I was eating on my own in an international hotel, he might have thought I was there for business other than music? And what would the two elderly aunts make of it all? I look over and the General smiles at me, with a glint in his eye.

My friends realise the situation is perhaps more serious than it first seemed and suggest a rescue plan. Staging a fake toilet or smoking break, they will escort me out of the dining hall whilst chatting casually, and I can then escape to my room. A last big sip of Riesling, and this is what we do. The General doesn't seem to take notice, so I make it safely to the hotel reception, thank the musicians profusely, and run up the stairs. I lock the door and fall onto the bed.

But just when I start to calm down, there is a sudden loud banging on my door. I decide to ignore it completely. After some time, and to my huge relief, I can hear the footsteps move away. I grab the phone and call reversed charges to my better half, explaining the whole saga at great length. Still unaware of the financial implications of this, it at least made me catch my breath and feel like myself again. I tried to use my Oma's technique of seeing it as a film, which helped somewhat. But sleeping didn't really happen that night.

The next morning, I go into the breakfast room and every waiter I pass bursts out laughing. When I get to my table, one of them comes up to me, telling me I hadn't signed for the dinner bill the night before, and that they'd come to my room to ask if I could do so. Ah, that would explain the knocking. Then, with a big grin on his face, he continues 'But we are very happy you did not get together with the General! He does this every year for his birthday and has quite a reputation. You are lucky you did not end up as his wife, as he is not getting any younger and wants to settle down!' Hilarity all round, I sign the bill and rush to that morning's rehearsal and the safe place that is Dvořák's music.

The whole of the rehearsal period with the orchestra was very positive, apart from, perhaps, my little *Figaro* moment. I guessed that the players had been in State employment which, even during the hardest of times, must have brought them at least a level of comfort and an ability to do a job that they loved.

I had been a bit nervous about my lack of experience when it came to a short rehearsal period with a good professional orchestra, but there was no need to be. One of my dilemmas was whether I should play through the Bruch Violin Concerto before the soloist joined us, or if that would be seen as a bit of an insult. The question was answered that afternoon, when the orchestra's own Principal Conductor came to do a rehearsal on Beethoven's Triple Concerto for the festival the following week. As the pianist would be conducting it from the keyboard, the orchestra had requested a pre-festival play through, so I thought I would probably get away with suggesting the same for the Bruch.

I watched the Beethoven rehearsal. The conductor made a lot of drastic musical decisions. Ritenuti, pauses and big dynamic gestures, not all of them indicated in the score, or suggested by the music itself. It surprised me, but I did also notice the wonderful sound he got from the players. I was about to leave when he came up to me and introduced himself. He again spoke good English and was personable in his manner. 'I have seen the rehearsal this morning, not bad, but you must ask much more for dynamic contrast!' It suddenly sounded quite stern. I was a bit taken aback, and briefly thanked him for the advice before stumbling out onto the street. The Leader was smoking a cigarette on the steps of the hall and said, 'You know, he is one of the great Maestros of our country', before wandering off.

It struck me. I should have shown a lot more respect and taken all the time in the world to let him teach me. I still beat myself up about not doing that. But at the time, being overwhelmed by all the experiences, I didn't always make the best decisions.

Concert day arrived, as did Gabriel Croitoru, the soloist for the Bruch. He was one of Romania's brightest musical stars, the loveliest man, and his playing was astounding. Technically flawless, but also with a passion that was really moving, even more so as he didn't seem to do anything over the top. It was just there, in his sound and in his being. He was the easiest to follow, and the concerto clicked together without any problems.

After the rehearsal he insisted on taking me out for lunch in the most expensive place in town. How could I say no?! I'd had real trouble trying to eat in restaurants that week. Or buy a phone card. Or indeed get train seats. (This was done by the Orchestral Manager in the end, who offered after hearing of my botched attempt). That side of being here had been very depressing and caused the reverse charge call bill to go up and up.

Gabriel never asked anything in the restaurant, he just barked orders around in the rudest tone. 'Are we ever going to get a menu, or what?' And it all came, with smiles and compliments. He explained that this was how people spoke. Being shy and polite got you nowhere. It was like people didn't understand the sentiment. I found it quite upsetting that shouting and being rude was the language of the outside world here, but it certainly fitted with my own experiences. The hotel and orchestra had been my safe places, but for the rest, I'd felt like a nuisance to everyone.

The concert that evening was a success. A full house with lots of young music students in the audience. I was brave and forced through my faster speeds, Gabriel's Bruch was out of this world, and Mozart was a happy mix of Brahms with a tiny bit of Beethoven thrown in. And it was fabulous for it. The players thanked me afterwards, and seemed genuinely positive, expressing hope that there would be a next time. The Leader and his front desk partner took time to tell me they had been impressed. They thought I had handled it all well and had felt in safe hands musically. Then they turned to each other and laughed, 'Even that Dvořák first movement was not too excruciatingly slow in the end, don't you think?' I took it all as a huge compliment.

When I was about to leave the hall, the nice young double bass player and second violinist, who had been chatty the whole week, ran after me to say how much they had enjoyed things. And that next time maybe they could show me the city. I felt bad, as I should have taken them out for a drink, something nobody there could really afford. My tiny embassy fee, in Dutch currency, was worth three months' salary there.

But it was as it was, and above all, I felt happy. Happy the concert was a good one and happy I had managed to hold my own musically and humanly. But the biggest relief was that I hadn't ended-up a General's wife.

The Wagenaar never did show up. I don't know if it is now a staple of the orchestra's mainstream repertoire, if it is still sitting at a border post somewhere, or if it was even sent in the first place. But I now do know that Romania had the highest reverse-charge call rates in Europe, the £250 bill causing a near-disownment by my parents-in-law. I was very ready to take the 8-hour train journey back to Hungary, and not be yelled at in the streets again for a good while. I wasn't sure if I'd be able to take a full week of that again.

‘Just before you go, why did you rehearse in French, when everyone in the orchestra speaks excellent English, and we always rehearse in English?’ the young violinist asks. I was such a dope…!

Wagenaar and Dutch composers

During my time in the UK, the question, 'Does Holland have any composers of its own?' was one that came up a lot. Homegrown British composers are aplenty, and enthusiastically celebrated in their concert halls. I was certainly familiar with the works of Elgar and Vaughan Williams, as well as a few snippets of Delius. But discovering the music of Finzi, Bliss, Walton, Rebecca Clarke and Grace Williams – all household names – had been wonderful. There would usually be a genuine sense of disbelief when I explained that in Holland, these composers are not nearly as mainstream as they are in the UK. But the counterargument was totally justifiable, hardly anyone had even heard of a single Dutch composer.

I would throw Orlando di Lasso into the ring, who strictly speaking was Flemish, but is someone the Renaissance buffs would still be impressed by. As well as our proper own Jan Pieterszoon Sweelinck, from Deventer, and of *Chromatic Fantasy* fame. But after that, the selection gets very small and rather niche.

It does throw up the interesting question as to why a country like the Netherlands, which was always at the forefront of innovation and business, doesn't boast a gallery of world-famous composers. It is true that from the late sixteenth century, Holland focused mainly on the visual arts, as a way to sell the new 'Republiek der Nederlanden' to the rest of the world. Call it advertising, or even propaganda, Frans Hals, Rembrandt and the famous land- and seascape painters like Ruysdael and the Van der Velde dynasty were all propelled into the international limelight.

Music didn't seem to be part of all this, and from that point in time a solid base for a 'music-creating' tradition was lacking. Another side to it might be that as a Republic, the Netherlands was always focused on 'looking out', again as a way to gain business, being the little country that it is. Creating personal identity through poetry and music seemed less crucial somehow. With the fiercely prudish Protestant church overseeing how Dutch life was lived, extravagant musical experiences like the flamboyant concerts that Mozart and Beethoven would organise, or opera, didn't really flourish until much later into the Romantic era, in the mid to late nineteenth century.

But when the Concertgebouw Orchestra was established in 1888, things changed. Amsterdam suddenly became a centre for the great musicians and composers to flock to and to show their art, not only to Holland, but to the rest of the world. Brahms and Mahler soon became famous regular visitors. And during this time, the 'creating' of music started to take off more. I remember being pleasantly surprised by the *Allegro for Three String Quartets*, by Johannes van Bree, dating from 1845, as well as the E Minor Symphony by Verhulst, another Johannes, from 1841. Mendelssohn and Schumann, eat your hearts out!

For me, two composers jump out of the pack, Alphons Diepenbrock and Johannes (what is it with that first name!?) Wagenaar.

Diepenbrock, who was born in 1862 in Amsterdam, was not a musician by training. He was brought up in a wealthy Catholic family, and the expectation was that he would enter a university rather than a conservatoire. And so, he went to study classics in Amsterdam, gaining his doctorate in 1888 with a dissertation, in Latin, on the life of the Spanish philosopher Seneca. That same year he became a teacher, a move that made him quickly realise that this was not the life for him, and he decided to devote himself primarily to music in 1894.

As a composer, he had been completely self-taught, creating a totally unique musical language which combined sixteenth century polyphony (maybe an ode to Sweelinck) with almost Wagnerian chromaticism. In later years, he added an impressionistic refinement, inspired by the music of Debussy and Ravel. Being a huge fan of the poetry of Goethe, Verlaine and Beaudelaire, he used it in abundance as the basis of his, mostly vocal, compositions.

In 1885, Diepenbrock married into properly posh circles, to (and I hope you are sitting down for this) Lady Wilhelmina Elisabeth Cornelia Petronella de Jong van Beek en Donk. No need for a Russian stage name there, thank you very much!

He mixed with the great and good, and could count Gustav Mahler, Richard Strauss and Arnold Schoenberg amongst his personal friends, with them showing their huge appreciation not only for his personal company but also for his growing musical output. He conducted many contemporary works at the Concertgebouw, including Mahler's Fourth Symphony, as well as pieces by Fauré and Debussy. Together with Wagenaar, his was one of the few Dutch names that was allowed to be added in golden letters to the famous gallery in the Concertgebouw: high praise indeed.

Throughout his life, Diepenbrock remained a part-time classics tutor, and published works on literature, painting, politics, philosophy and religion. So much so that his musical skills were often overlooked in wider Holland. Nonetheless, he was a very much respected figure within prominent musical circles and his works continue to be performed all over the world, something I keenly rub in when discussing Dutch composers with English friends and colleagues.

His two stand-out works are the deeply evocative tone poems *Hymne an die Nacht* and *Im Grossen Schweigen*. Both have been recorded by the Concertgebouw Orchestra under Riccardo Chailly, and the Residence Orchestra under Hans Vonk.

I was very lucky that the Dutch Embassy in London invited me to record a selection of Diepenbrock's songs. Working with the wonderful Dutch mezzo-soprano Joke De Vin, these CD recordings are up there as some of my proudest achievements. How Diepenbrock puts Beaudelaire's *Invitation au voyage* to sound, pulling us into a dream of desire, ecstasy and imagination like no one else has (not even Duparc), and how Joke would vocally embody this...It still gives me goosebumps when I listen to it.

In my opinion, Diepenbrock is a true world class composer, who was possibly held back by that Dutch unwillingness to be too proud of their own 'countrymen of culture'. And maybe this links with Haitink's thoughts on how tough it could be as a Dutch musician in Holland. If you are used to an environment where non-Dutch names make up the spectrum of composers, and those golden names of the Concertgebouw gallery, then maybe it is harder to be accepted as a Dutch one. And possibly that also spills over into the world of performers and conductors.

Wagenaar's music was suggested to me by my agent at the time, who had helped organise the concert trip to Transylvania. The massive tone poems of Diepenbrock would have been too much to aim for in my short week there, but the overtures of Wagenaar were the perfect length, impactful, and provided a nice testament of that Dutch romantic musical era.

Wagenaar's start in life was a bit of a scandal. He was born in Utrecht, but out of wedlock, not something that was the 'done thing' in those days. Wagenaar's parents were from different social strata: his father was an aristocrat, whilst his mother was of a much humbler background. For this reason, they were not married and Wagenaar received his mother's family name.

Whilst he was unhappy that his parents never married, Wagenaar was by no means neglected by his father. Little Johan didn't start formal education in music until he was 13, but it then took off for real with rigorous lessons in piano, organ, violin, theory, and composition. The well-known composer Richard Hol taught him personally, and in 1892, he went to study with Brahms' good friend Heinrich von Herzogenberg in Berlin, specifically taking lessons in counterpoint.

A few years before, in 1888, Wagenaar's life had moved towards the place of my own musical professional training. He succeeded Richard Hol as organist of the Utrecht Cathedral, became a teacher at the music school in 1896, and then the school's Director in 1904. The very spot where we gave our lunchtime concerts at the Conservatoire, and where my friend was crowned the successor of Liberace, of candelabra fame.

He soon received an appointment with the Utrecht Municipal Orchestra (Utrechts Stedelijk Orkest). The same orchestra that at an early concert for schools had opened our young souls to the magic of sound with De Falla's *Three Cornered Hat*. Rounds of unjustifiable and unforgivable funding cuts had caused this wonderful orchestra to bite the dust many years ago. What their playing did for us as youngsters was truly inspiring and instilled a sense of self-confidence that only music can. 'We are alive, and it is awesome', or something along those lines. Governments hacking away at these opportunities is totally shortsighted. But I know I am preaching to the converted here.

Between 1919 and 1937, Wagenaar was Director of the Royal Conservatoire in The Hague. His pupils there included Peter van Anrooy, Leon Orthel, Clara Wildschut and Willem Pijper, who all went on to become prominent Dutch composers. Wagenaar's own compositions included operas, cantatas, organ music, and orchestral works. The music of Berlioz had a modest influence on his language, but Richard Strauss was the real, and at times quite obvious, inspiration.

Wagenaar died in The Hague in 1941, the second year of the Second World War for occupied Holland. Hitler attempted to use culture to spread his own perverted sense of glory, but in doing so, he unintentionally provided many occupied people with an outlet, and something upon which they could project their own emotions. My grandmother describes in her war diaries how Hitler's birthday concert in Amsterdam (Beethoven 9, under Willem Mengelberg), provided great courage and hope through the words of the *Ode to Joy*. And Wagenaar was just about still able to contribute to that.

Wagenaar might not have enjoyed the same international respect as Diepenbrock, but his orchestral works are popular repertoire in Holland and abroad, especially his *Taming of the Shrew* overture, which is indeed a fantastic piece. There are several recordings of it out there by prominent Dutch and international orchestras and conductors. And the same goes for *Cyrano de Bergerac*. *Don Juan*'s spirit might be gazing down on this overture-come-tone poem, but Wagenaar's own voice and ingenuity are present throughout, and it proves a true advocate for the music written in my little homeland at that time.

It was a great opportunity to rehearse and perform *Cyrano* with the orchestra in Bristol, and his shorter tone poem, *El Cid*, in Berkshire, and the music made a real impact. I got my own back! To be able to take it to the Transylvanian State Philharmonic, a respected international orchestra, and spread the word even further, would have been the cherry on the cake. It is still sad that Romanian customs had other ideas...

La Forza del Comitato

> *'A good conductor ought to be a good chauffeur; the qualities that make the one also make the other. They are concentration, an incessant control of attention, and presence of mind; the conductor only has to add a little sense of music.'*
> *Sergei Rachmaninoff*

(It must be remembered that Rachmaninoff was a fanatical driver of fast cars and later speedboats!)

The moment of truth was getting closer, and I was frantically trying to remember everything I had been instructed to do. Make sure the voicing of the parallel thirds was correct. Make sure the lines were flowing and with a proper legato, which was hard, this being a xylophone setting on a tiny and very plastic keyboard. Make sure I started playing at all, which sounds simple, but was not.

On very short notice, a lot of cuts had been made and extra repeat bars added. And this was only one of the many parts I was trying to cover this evening. Rather last minute, the final rehearsal before the concert in fact, I had been given missing harp and percussion parts, including a drumkit flourish, which was new territory for me. (I knew those quick repeated note studies Alan had prescribed all those years ago would prove useful again, be it quite removed from their original purpose of enabling Ravel's *Albarado del Grazioso*). All these things came with serious challenges. Changed bar numbers and instrument codes to remember and to press whilst trying to count simultaneously, bringing with it the real risk of a harpsichord taking centre stage in the middle of a Johann Strauss waltz.

Then there was our conductor, who seemed quite unaware of the limitations of my 80 centimetres of fake piano, on wobbly legs and without a sustain pedal. He had spent a long time making his worries about my brave attempts known, from the articulation to the specific tone colour. I had considered sharing my own concerns about the toy keyboard, but I was always taught never to talk back to the person in charge.

At least my fingers were still able to move after the many hours of this rehearsal. No such luxury for the lips of the brass players. There had been endless goes at their sections that morning, with urgent requests for more sound, clearer articulation ('front of mouth, bitte') and the deeper meaning of some particular staccato markings. 'Let's try that again', or, 'Versuchen wir das noch einmal!' was a line that had become a curse. We all got slightly worried, as it was now less than an hour before the concert, leaving no recovery time.

When the session finally finished, we were hastily given some last-minute changes to the start of the second half. Whilst people were packing up and talking amongst themselves, the Maestro told us that the opening of *Also Sprach* would be repeated, after a comic verbal introduction. This was not as written in the programme but would work very well. The *Blue Danube* Waltz would then follow after that repeat. People nodded politely and rushed off to a much-needed hour of relaxation and desperate, but in vain, embouchure recovery.

I looked around and took in the glorious setting that is Düsseldorf's Tonhalle. Concert halls don't get much more glamorous than this. Originally built as a planetarium, its transformation is simply stunning. The massive dome is now covered in blue lights, giving a mesmerising 'sky-at-night' atmosphere. In it sits a very spacious light wooden stage, and the audience seats rake up in a three-level gallery construction. The acoustics are second to none, as are the backstage facilities. The conductor's dressing room is huge, with not one, but two grand pianos, a sumptuous leather sofa and glorious views of the Rhine. They treat their musicians well here.

I counted my bars, and tried to make large Dutch fingers find tiny plastic keys. 'Legato, just 'look' legato!', I was thinking. Which I did. And without too many obvious clashes, my sections came out quite respectably.

The second half arrived, and with it, the dark rumblings of the iconic *2001: A Space Odyssey* music. What would Richard Strauss have made of the fact that everyone in the world knows the first two minutes of his *Also Sprach Zarathustra*, whilst the next hour of this masterpiece is only appreciated by serious classical music fanatics? He would probably have loved it, would've had it copyrighted separately and would've realised that it was more than most other composers could boast about.

The trumpets start their motif, quiet but secure, building to the first two-note resolution, followed by the timpani. (Thank God these were the real deal, and not a keyboard version!) Then the second round, with trumpets now building like a threat almost and the resolution also bolder, before it all unleashes at the end of this short opening passage. It had been a success, and all lips seemed just about able to hold the sound together.

The spoken comedic dialogue follows, but it is of more epic proportions than a performance of the complete tone poem would have been. After about ten minutes of it, the conductor looks at the percussion and bass sections, who look back at him in great surprise. One of the players suddenly remembers the repeat instructions, grabs an implement, and starts rumbling anything that is within reach. The top strings abruptly abort their high tremolos that open the *Blue Danube* Waltz, looking very worried.

One lone trumpet, who had actually marked the order of proceedings in his part, starts the motif, with no lip left, in a shaky half tone, only just clinging on to his top notes and barely able to produce any sound. More noticeable, though, is the loud swearing from the French horn section behind me, realising that they had totally forgotten that it was *Also Sprach* again, and were now frantically trying to find the music for it. Eventually all players are on board, but not a single top note survives.

When, at the end of the evening, the orchestra is ordered to play the complete *James Bond Medley* again as an encore, for the third time that concert, there is hardly any brass audible anymore. The concert had lasted over three hours, and nothing was left of the poor players. We learned again that the art of getting the best out of musicians, when it matters most, is a fine one.

That said, these joint concerts were always a total delight. The partnership between Reading (Berkshire) and Düsseldorf is a testament to incredible human resolve. Set up after the Second World War, when Reading provided a haven for children from the near-destroyed German city, it is still proving to be relevant today. Brexit and the Covid pandemic brought people closer together through cultural partnerships like theirs, showing once again how vital music can be. Or creating poetry, or visual art, or anything that allows one to express oneself and share.

Through the Berkshire and Düsseldorf orchestras, I was reminded time and again how making music and 'being' together through that process makes an essential difference. Life hits hard at times, but having that golden gift makes things better, easier. It makes you feel less alone, like a huge hug, or a shoulder to lean on. It should never be underestimated.

Musical Director of the Berkshire orchestra was one of the positions that I had taken up after leaving college. Andre Previn said that being able to work with what he called 'community orchestras' was an ideal way to learn repertoire and to hone the skill of being a useful conductor.

The UK stands out for the high level of its non-professional music making. Choirs, orchestras, opera companies, there are many, and on a good day they can give professional equivalents a run for their money. It still seems to be a vital part of people's everyday life, and many professionally trained players and conductors are working with these organisations, providing fantastic concerts, attended by large audiences.

Whilst the assistant auditions and early professional engagements were happening, I had also applied for three of these posts: a London opera group and non-professional orchestras based in Bristol and Reading. Not only could this provide me with crucial experience, but also a much-needed income. Looking back, it was funny how the essential character of each group was clear from the very first time we crossed paths.

During my try-out rehearsal for the opera group, the chorus and I had ended up in stitches when trying to find more theatrical and convincing ways to sing a 'laughing' episode of one of the excerpts from *Orpheus in the Underworld* (Offenbach, not Monteverdi, I should probably add). Experimenting with more realistic 'techniques' set us all off and created a positive bond there and then.

What I hadn't expected though was the measures of ambition, at times near obsessive, displayed by some of the principal singers. We would often get people apply whose voices seemed of a high professional standard. The old and wise company bass once told me they would always wonder why someone of such vocal calibre would audition for a non-paying company, but that they'd normally find out within a few weeks of rehearsing. And invariably, we did!

The first event I was involved in was an informal soirée, with people of the company singing songs and arias. They were often tipsy affairs, with guests drinking copiously and enjoying each other's company, whilst raising some extra funds for the group. I sight-read happily through wildly eclectic repertoire, until one very stressed looking gentleman approached me, apologising that he had brought his own accompanist as they had rehearsed his aria together for a long time. He couldn't risk being derailed by someone he hadn't worked with before. It immediately became clear that for him, this was not a fun evening at all, but a deadly serious presentation of his skills. He was a strong singer, but his levels of angst would make things very tough in production rehearsals.

And in my years with the company there were a huge number of similar personalities. Voices to drool over, but lacking a total ability to count to two, three or four (in Verdi, their favourite, more is not often needed). Or high stress levels resulting in near accidents on stage.

For four nights in a row, a middle-aged and vocally challenged bass, who was somehow singing the young love interest (he was a committee elder and brought in his own audience – need we say more?), managed to fall through the tiny space between the steps and the stage. He would clamber back up with his costume wildly out of place, and the rest of the cast would struggle not to lose it, either with hysterical laughter or with a totally justified urge to throttle him.

Not being able to remember words, or stage directions, or both, was a regular occurrence with principals and chorus members alike. As was a ruthless ambition to be 'The Star of the Show'. Manipulating over which nights they could share their glory, patronising and intimidating colleagues, especially those who would be doubling their part: it was an over-the-top version of the professional world it seemed.

I remember painful discussions about who could sing which parts, with some of the hopefuls totally unaware of their lack of ability, or suitability for a character. The young and flirtatious Mercedes in *Carmen* at the tender age of 75? Even I started to doubt this, as the arguments and 'persuading' letters grew more plentiful. 'The Committee': it was to become a whole new aspect of music making.

But the experience it gave me was priceless. Life lessons in people management, but also the art of being able to musically follow, well, anything really. People singing too soon, not singing at all, singing double speed, singing half speed, or skipping whole pages of the score. I developed a pretty much foolproof technique for recitative conducting, making sure I was always staying ahead of the singers in their sections, during pauses for the orchestra. Beat through their bars like crazy, and 'hang' there with the upbeat, having the 'Not yet please!' left arm ready to stifle every opportunistic attempt by anyone to vocally gatecrash before it was their time.

One of the best voices we ever had was a young tenor, who had already been given small parts with the main professional companies in the UK. But this was a huge leading role in a Verdi opera. On the first night he failed to appear for his long recitative and aria in the opening Act. There was nothing we could do, except to hope that the Director would drag him out of his dressing room. Except that this was the night the young and very ambitious Director couldn't be there. Another compromise that seemed odd to me, but which had been agreed to for some reason. The orchestral accompaniment was literally one chord every five bars, for pages on end. I started to accelerate through them, to have at least some sound going on.

The soprano thought that improvised on-stage action might also help things, and promptly walked straight through the wall of the house to get a drink of water from a non-existent kitchen sink, leaving her confused-looking father behind on the garden bench.

By the end of what would have been the recitative, there was a loud noise, and our hero ran to the front of the stage, knocking over two unsuspecting elderly chorus ladies in the process. He started his aria (which sounded very glorious, I will admit), and we moved on like nothing had happened. Afterwards he apologised, saying that he couldn't get his cloak on properly, and had been worried he might miss his cue. I still don't know if he ever realised that he had missed the whole of the recitative, or if he just thought that in this way, he didn't have to memorise it. He was ill for his second night, so we never found out.

But there were many fantastic singers we were privileged to work with, and who have gone on to successful professional careers. And the repertoire was huge. The warhorses like *Carmen*, Verdi favourites like *Forza* and *Macbeth* and *Nabucco*, Gounod's *Faust*, the list goes on. But it was the lesser-known operas that stand out for me. Britten's *Gloriana*, Tchaikovsky's *Queen of Spades* and Walton's little opera *The Bear*, they all were revelations.

After 10 years it was time to move on, but I am happy to say that the central people of the company are still some of my closest friends. Over many bottles of red wine, we often spend long evenings laughing and reminiscing about the adventures that were. And the experience enabled me to be part of some wonderful professional opera projects in the years that were ahead. But those will one day make a book of their own.

The two orchestras which had allowed me to become their Musical Director, as it is called in this circuit, could not have been more different in identity and atmosphere.

I remember taking the train to Bristol, and whilst getting closer to my destination, a feeling of optimism kicking in. The countryside was beautiful, and the train station and vistas of Bath made me think that not living in London might even be an option, something which had been a blasphemous thought up until then.

Even though Bristol Parkway was less glamorous in its setting, my lift was friendly and chatty, as was the committee welcoming me to the rehearsal venue. I had been asked to prepare the first and second movements of Saint-Saëns' Organ Symphony, a piece I was, and still am, very fond of. The orchestra's present conductor was there which surprised me slightly, but which didn't bring any awkwardness. She was a classy lady with years of experience and seemed very positive about the prospect of being able to help choose the best new person for the job.

The orchestra were a very happy bunch it seemed, with a lot of smiles wherever I looked. I played through the second movement and was impressed by how keen they were to go into more musical and technical detail. After 20 minutes, I realised that the trombones were already there, having been called for the start of the rehearsal even though the second movement (which they weren't in) had been planned for that time. I remembered sitting in our little youth orchestra, waiting and waiting whilst the conductor went through every possible fingering and bowing with the string section, whilst our lives were flashing before our eyes. (I should add that it took many years before I realised that not every orchestra has third violins, this hopefully telling you something about the desperate need for those instructions).

I always tried to keep everyone busy, especially if a schedule had been created, and people knew in advance what sections were going to be rehearsed and when. At the same time, if you play a triangle, or the trombone in a Beethoven symphony, you know there is some waiting to be done. The players here certainly did understand that and seemed to enjoy observing the work we were doing. I quickly changed to the first movement, and again found a real connection with everyone. They were perhaps not the most amazing players technically, but there was a good sound, and a big improvement in a short time. But most of all, a real musical happiness somehow. The interview with the committee afterwards felt more like an exchange of ideas on how the orchestra could move forward musically, but also publicity wise.

I raced back to catch my London train and felt very relieved. But also had the realisation that positivity in making music together was key for me. Being able to go through that process with a sense of being a team was a great thing, and something I was also good at cultivating. In that sense, it had been like coming home. When the news came that the orchestra had decided they wanted to offer me the job, I was very happy about it.

The experience of the Berkshire audition was very different. What had struck me initially was them describing themselves back then as 'one of the leading amateur orchestras in the country'. This set the bar of expectation quite high, as there are some astoundingly good non-professional orchestras in the UK. Then, I was told that the orchestra never stuck with one conductor for more than three or four years, as they felt there was nothing to gain from the same person after that. This statement did set a few more alarm bells ringing.

The old Reading train station might make Bristol Parkway feel like Grand Central, but the town is close to London, so it would make for a quick commute every week. We arrived at the rehearsal venue, and I was put in a little waiting room whilst the candidate before me took their audition. I could just see through the window of the door and realised that I knew him from college. He was the young star conductor who had graduated the year before me and seemed to be making promising steps towards a strong career. Things didn't sound amazing though, and there were long silences in between the music. After half an hour, he came out, recognised me and sat down looking angry. 'Well, I never want to conduct them again, and I will let them know as soon as I am home', was his quick assessment of the situation. He left immediately, hardly filling me with lots of positivity about the next 45 minutes.

I had been given the *Royal Hunt and Storm* from the *Troyans* by Berlioz to conduct, which comes with a lot of cross rhythm issues. Four against six, and three over four but over two bars. It is a bit of a minefield but would also give me something specific to work on. The moment I stepped into the room, in my blue Boston shirt (sadly not Greek-pressed this time), I could feel that there seemed to be a 'player ranking system' in place. The strings were lovely, if a little timid. Their professional leader was a kind and jolly man. The woodwind players, however, gave off a very different vibe, as did the brass sections apart from the trumpets, who again seemed shy.

I start the piece, and after 10 bars the principal oboist stops the playing and tells me that I am slower than their own conductor. I explain that this is always something that might happen in an audition, but that I thought the 'non troppo' marking was essential to give that march-like feel, as opposed to a race. And that being able to adapt to a slightly slower speed now would only make their faster final version stronger. (My time at the opera group, dealing with the occasional diva, had already taught me a lot and given me a comprehensive repertoire of 'come backs'). Some violinists look up at me with smiles and admiration. Not so the oboist, but she decides to leave it alone.

When we come to the cross rhythms, I can't detect any of them actually happening, or even being attempted. I stop and ask the main sections to play their particular patterns. 'We have been told to just leave them out, as it is too difficult for us', is the unexpected reply. I decide to see if we could lift the spirits a bit and suggest that we could still give it a go, by practising things in a different way. If anything, it would make for a good general exercise. And to everyone's amazement, the rhythms clicked. A round of applause for the trumpets, who nailed it the moment they started listening to the basses and not to the woodwind. The oboist intervenes. 'This is a waste of time, as we are not going to have them in, so could you please continue?', was the harsh instruction. I give her a smile and decide to go with the flow, even if it is an icy one.

The strings still seemed to hold back, so I take a little time to see if we can make a difference. I ask the Leader to demonstrate a few things, and soon a freedom starts to kick in. Genuinely excited, I applaud them and am surprised that most of the woodwind and brass players spontaneously join me, whistling and all. Positivity and confidence, the two things that were lacking, but which now start to flow. And having fun too, it is so crucial. A few violinists look at me suspiciously, but don't speak up.

We play on, but when I can't hear the French horns at all, and ask for a little more sound, the fourth player gives me a death stare and states that it says 'pianissimo' in the music. A famous Rotterdam Philharmonic reply quickly comes into my mind, and to the rescue. 'Well maybe, but we would like to actually hear you play pianissimo'. I was not proud to use a stolen phrase, but needs must. More daggers and mumblings from that corner. We move towards the end of my audition, and the novelty, for me, of some players constantly feeling the need to question perfectly reasonable observations.

The level of playing was not particularly higher than in Bristol, even though there seemed to be more professionally trained players here. It just didn't sound very good, certainly not to the point where they could justify stating they were one of the leading amateur orchestras in the UK. But the strings had been playing their hearts out by the end, and that made me feel positive. I totally understood my college friend's sentiment, however, and was also considering if this was the right orchestra for me to conduct.

Having challenged some of what seemed to be the leading figures in the ranks, I totally expected that I would not be asked back for a second audition, and I would have been quite happy with that. But to my amazement the phone call from the Chairman comes the following day, with him telling me that after the players' vote, the second round of auditions would be cancelled if I was happy to take up the position from the following term. 'Had it been a test?', I remember thinking. I decided that whatever it was, the positive outcome was enough reason to give it a go, and let's face it, they would ask me to leave in a few short years anyway!

In Bristol, there had been some concern about me having to travel down from London every week, as well as being a young conductor who might move on quite quickly. But when I explained to them that my UK family base was not far off, and that I intended to spend at least three more years learning repertoire and gaining vital work experience, those worries seemed to be quickly wiped away. And it would become the routine for many more than three years. Travelling down on Monday afternoons, spending the night in Bristol and travelling back to London on Tuesday.

I often stayed at the house of one of the senior horn players. Nigel was the son of Lesley Boosey, putting the Boosey into *Boosey and Hawkes*. He was very charming, and my times there were a treasure. He and his wife Penelope offered a real home to me, and Nigel's family stories and experiences from the days of the publishing house's glory period were a treat. Personal recollections of Britten, Rachmaninoff, Kodaly and so many more, brought that world back to life, and gave me a lot of inspiration. Being a wise man, at times he would also give me a bit of advice on how to handle a situation. 'Never indulge' he once told me in the car, after a rather fraught rehearsal at which I had become a bit of a diva. Those words still come back to me regularly. He was so right: the risk lies just around the corner.

Our first term was as positive as I had hoped for, and it was clear that the feeling was mutual. We worked hard on Tchaikovsky's Fourth Symphony (always a bigger beast than you remember), Elgar's Cello Concerto and Verdi's *La Forza Del Destino* overture. (I tackled the full opera only years later and realised that for me, the overture is more than enough. Apart from one sliver of light relief (in the form of the slightly dotty Padre Melitone, who feeds soup to the poor, only to be ridiculed by them), there is just misery, and a record number of dead people at the closing chords. With our particular cast though, that aspect had not been an unwelcome one...)

The resulting concert in Bristol was a great success, and the orchestra played their socks off. It might have been a bit rough and ready in places, but the passion and rich sound told me we could do wonderful things in the years to come. And I had loved the process of having weekly rehearsals to grow together towards the performance and really become part of this musical family. I was starting to realise where I was most happy and successful in my conducting life.

Back in Berkshire, it had become clear that the audition vibe had not been a test, but a true reflection of the orchestra's hierarchy, bringing a whole new and challenging aspect to being Musical Director of an orchestra like this. Whilst in Bristol we were working positively towards the future (raising the playing level, attracting new members, finding new venues and upgrading the publicity), things in Berkshire were much more complicated.

I had discovered that some players in the orchestra used to be paid to play but had eventually accepted to be subscription members just like everyone else. This had led to the two-tier feel that I had experienced during the audition, and which had become more noticeable (and more counterproductive) in the time beyond it. The string players in general seemed nervous about playing out and being 'free', whilst the small group, the clique, gave off an air of being superior to everyone, including the conductor. Their playing standards didn't really justify this attitude, and it made rehearsals tough at times. The moment I would suggest anything about their own playing, they would bite back defensively. And when I gave the strings the time they needed to gain confidence, there seemed to be resentment.

Whilst in Bristol we had to tighten things up and add more discipline to the very positive and open atmosphere, in Berkshire, it was the opposite. I encouraged a more sociable break time, and played a lot of longer stretches to get the orchestra to feel as one and to relax into the music. I added more jokes to lighten the tension, and lavished compliments on the players when it all sounded good. This triggered a rather dramatic response from 'the clique', who started sending me individual letters, ordering me to be stricter in telling people off, and even asking players to play passages individually, as if to shame them. In the orchestra's Leader David, though, I found a true ally, who gave a lot of instruction and support to the section. He also, unintentionally, was the trigger for a big, positive, turnaround for the orchestra a year later. And we still thank him for that great act of humanity.

One of the main principles I had come to abide by is that you should never tread on the toes of the section leaders. Don't go in with preconceived bowing ideas, that is what the Leader is there for. Just instruct clearly and musically. After a botched attempt to learn to play the violin in my teens, I knew very little about how to make the instrument sound good, which I think helped me in achieving that principle. David taught me a huge amount, by demonstrating different bowings, different techniques, and even fingerings, constantly asking me which of the resulting sounds I would prefer. After many years, I am now able to add more detail to my requests to the strings. Even so, my first port of call will always be the Leader. But being able to nudge is certainly a great tool.

With growing confidence, the sound of the orchestra was improving all the time. But as this seemed to be a threat to the superiority of the clique, their criticism became nastier and more personal. To stay sane and positive, I could always fall back on my work with the Bristol orchestra. But now also on the ever-stronger positive feedback I was receiving from increasing numbers of players in Berkshire itself. It enabled me to regain confidence in my ability and to trust my gut instinct.

What didn't help things, but what certainly made them more colourful, was that the Chairman at that time was having many romantic liaisons within the orchestra, and most of the ladies involved had ended up on the committee. Jilly Cooper would have loved it. One in particular was very keen to share dubious details of the physical relations she was having with him, as well as throw the other objects of his affection under the bus. Very little effective orchestra business was carried out, as most ideas would be booed off in fits of personal spite.

As we worked on changing the identity of the orchestra, the old committee fell apart bit by bit, and the Chairman decided to step down. But more importantly, the silent majority of players were starting to find their own voice. Eventually, it all came to a head in a very operatic manner: *Force of Destiny* at its most powerful!

Act One

Location: *The scene is set at a beautiful stately home just outside Reading. Lush gardens, on a balmy summer's evening, the concert just finished. Main characters in position (with sadly no dotty soup monk anywhere to be seen).*

And: **Action:**

David (probably a tenor):

> *'How awful was that harpsichord playing which totally ruined the concerto?! The harpsichord must have been an IKEA flat-pack version, with the assembling of it having gone terribly wrong!'*

Stephan (probably a baritone):

> *'We mustn't speak now!'*

[**Stage direction:** frantic gesturing with head, as the culprit of the harpsichord playing, who is also the clique leader's husband, is standing only inches away from an oblivious David and he has heard everything.]

[**Music:** Verdi's three 'Destiny' chords sound loudly.]

David (not understanding Stephan's signals, and being very excited):

> *'The man can't even find a middle C!'*

[**Stage direction:** Stephan and the culprit's eyes meet; culprit leaves the stage into the darkness of the night. Stephan brings David the bad news of what just unfolded.]

[**Music:** The three 'Destiny' chords sound again.]

And thus, it all exploded.

Poisonous letters from the culprit to David (quite possibly written with the help of a local fortune teller from a dark past), came flying. These were followed by one hell of an AGM, which, lasting until gone midnight, unfolded like the orchestra's own *Un ballo in maschera*. The clique of conspirators misjudged the general feeling and were forced to stick with their threat to leave if the head of the Leader wasn't handed to them on

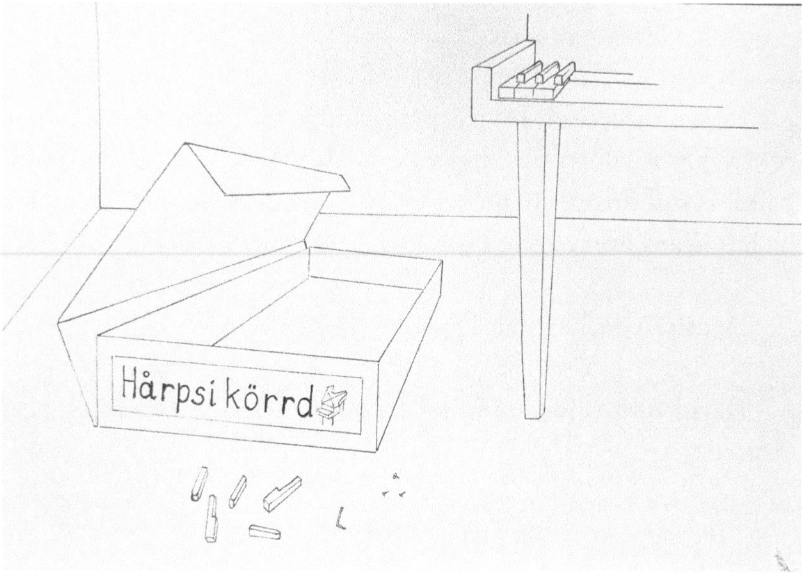

a plate (which it wasn't). And just like the opera itself, suddenly there were five fewer characters, be it not killed off, but who had retreated into their self-inflicted exile.

[**Stage direction:** The curtain rattles down to dramatic orchestral flourishes.]

It was the big turning point, and from that moment on, the level of playing and positivity shot up. I had learned the hard way that there was so much more to being Musical Director than just running rehearsals and conducting concerts. Or perhaps I had cared too much, and simply got involved where my predecessor had not. Through tireless hard work by the new committee members, and a much-strengthened optimism from the overwhelming majority of players, it felt like we could now conquer the world, both musically and in life spirit. They go hand in hand, after all; they maybe even equal each other.

On their best days the Berkshire orchestra could reach a strong playing level. Mahler's Second Symphony, joined by the Düsseldorf orchestra, was one of the highlights, as was their gutsy performance of Rachmaninoff's *Symphonic Dances*. Although the sight of the trombonist, to whom life had not always been kind, mooning the audience when his trousers started sliding down as he arrived late on stage for a concert, in the middle of the overture, is one that will never leave me. Or indeed the people who were in the audience that day.

It is fair to say that, until the end of my time at Berkshire, there were still times when I had to fight against the negative voices of a small number of people who thought they knew better. But then this is probably inevitable when working with a large organisation like a symphony orchestra. I am proud I refused to give in until my very last concert, knowing how good the orchestra was now sounding, and feeling a positive energy around me from the vast majority, which was in stark contrast to those early years. And there is no doubt that continued good times are ahead!

The Brahms Second Symphony that was my last concert with them was one of the orchestra's finest performances and made me feel proud and sad in equal measure. It had been an eventful ride. 27 years of it and nearly a quarter of a century more than I would initially have been allowed at the time of my audition. But of all the orchestras I had conducted, this was the one that built my confidence the most, not just as a musician, but maybe even more so as a 'committee-counteractor'. *Contrastatore del Comitato.*

The Mariposa Press Musical Dictionary: Index of Common Committee Personalities

Any of these can, and most likely will, appear in an organisation such as yours. Where appropriate and deemed helpful, a short case study is provided.

1. The Chairman who knows most of the committee members more intimately than is productive for committee matters.

— No need for extra explanation.

2. The Chairman who says they are acting on behalf of the underdog, when they aren't really. Known to:

– Drag players into this underdog role, even when they don't wish to be.

– Not listen.

– Mention 'what people have told them' a lot (even if there is little evidence that anyone actually has), using this to push their own agenda through.

– Not listen.

– Use membership or committee votes like an exam, with definite right or wrong answers.

– Not listen.

– Be delightfully unaware of anything concerning the above.

3. The Contract-Obsessed Secretary. Known to:

– Display an overdeveloped, near-obsessive, ability to dream up totally unrealistic disaster scenarios.

4. The Bullying Secretary/Concert Manager (also applicable to any of the above positions). Known to:

– Manipulate the fact that the one thing English people want to avoid is a 'situation'.

– Get their way because they know that it is easier for people to agree than to risk having to be part of a 'discussion'.

– Use the 'I am loud, so I am right' mantra, until a Dutch conductor with a strong sense of justice arrives.

!!WARNING!! Can get nasty in the aftermath!

5. The Waffling General Member with too much time on their hands. Known to:

– Drag-out meetings to five times their intended length, and make colleagues want to say and do things to them that they really shouldn't.

**If you find yourself in need of help or advice when confronted with any of the above, don't phone us. We only published the list.*

****It must be stressed that the above list is usually only a tiny minority of individuals in any orchestra. The much bigger, and much more positive majority make the organisation what it is, and this should always be remembered whenever dealing with the above characters. And remember, never indulge!*

In Bristol, we weren't immune either, but any nonsense was always dealt with quickly and in a positive, 'moving forward' spirit. For me, it was a joy to have to tone things down musically, rather than push for more. The real breakthrough came when we decided to move our concerts from a nice church in the suburbs to one of the city's main concert venues, St George's. It brought a financial risk, but at the same time we would be joining the more ambitious orchestras that regularly performed there. Bristol has a huge non-pro-orchestral scene, too huge you might think, and it is often a case of 'keep up or bow out'. We were now ready to bring high standard classical music to as many people as possible.

For our first concert there, it was Dvořák's Seventh Symphony again, a piece that seems to be a milestone vehicle for me. With the added pressure of being on the main stage in town, the rehearsals were more intense than they had been, but the playing level was going up week by week. It was a proud moment when the orchestra sounded the best they had ever done, to a near full house, and with rave reactions afterwards. A new bar had been set, and in the years to come, the orchestra kept rising to every occasion.

All the time, I realised more and more that I had found my 'thing'. Managing to combine my experience and craft, built up from extensive training and fieldwork, with being able to share my love for music with people who were there for that very reason. Sometimes professionally trained, but often not, combining a real personal passion with their busy working lives. What struck me with all these groups was the high level of musicality, even if the technical standards were at times less so. We could work on the musical detail, the composer's intentions, emotions, and phrasing, and people got it. And more importantly, wanted to get it. Being able to go on this journey with everyone made it very much a team effort, conductor included. And that was what I loved and excelled at.

Previn had said that making a pro-orchestra play well is 'peanuts', but to get a community orchestra to sound good is where the challenge lies. I have learned that he deliberately generalised here, but also came to realise what he really meant. I guess you can make a much bigger difference with these community orchestras. But I also learned that you are only of value if you have anything to show for yourself. Often when things are not as tight as they can be, I stop conducting altogether, to make people listen, and without fail they then nail it. And that is a reminder for us as conductors, that orchestras don't need us for them to just function. But if we have the goods, we can turn that 'functioning' into something extraordinary and important, and that stands for pro-orchestras and amateur orchestras alike.

Some of the best non-professional concerts I was lucky to conduct were those with the Bristol Concert Orchestra. A powerful *Dream of Gerontius*, and a very punchy and dramatic *Petrushka*. But it is Mahler's Ninth Symphony with them that has stayed with me the most. It hadn't been easy, as some players found the musical language and technical demands too daunting to begin with. But over time you could feel everyone becoming part of this emotional 'farewell to life'. They were probably the hardest, yet most rewarding ten weeks of rehearsing we ever had. The concert was of another level. Every single player was completely committed technically, but also adding an extra layer of something much more. It all seemed to come from one huge, combined soul. To be able to share that experience with them brought tears to my eyes. On stage even. Something I don't do.

I conducted regular professional projects during all these years, from insane opera festivals to chamber orchestra tours and engagements with more regular outfits. And they were rewarding. But I missed that team-feel at times. 'We did this together!'

I now realise that my need for that had made me lazy about finding auditions, taking on a pianist job at an opera house in Germany, or throwing myself into the competition circuit. And as the years passed, I grew out of the age-group for whom this was a realistic trajectory.

I had found what I loved to do, and what brought all my qualities together. No regrets, just a proud happiness, and sense of 'us'.

Mahler and goulash

> *'The two things you can't fake are good food and good music.'*
> *Etta James*

In Richard Osborne's wonderful book *Conversations with Karajan*, there is a lovely section where the two discuss the symphonies of Gustav Mahler. Karajan observes that in the Ninth, there is an element of catastrophe, like in his Sixth, but also great beauty and a sense of harmony with death. 'Coming to the end of this symphony is one of the hardest tasks in all conducting', he poignantly states.

Karajan's work on it with the Berlin Philharmonic was spread out over four years. First the 1979 LP recording, followed by a series of concerts in 1982, combined with the final live recording for CD. That last version still stands today as one of the towering and most crushing interpretations of all time. Karajan says that he was 'madly, madly involved with the work, to the extent that when it was all done, and this is one of the few works I would say this of, I would never dare to touch it again.'

Osborne tells Karajan that he was there at the 1982 Salzburg performance, and that the experience was so emotionally overwhelming that he had to leave his dinner reservation, as he was not able to eat. Karajan then shares that it was the same for him. And that 'that thing happens only once in a lifetime.'

The offloading and unwinding of emotional intensity after a major concert experience, and indeed the whole build-up to it as well, is one of the great rewards in life. Food always seems to have been the best way to get there. From Mozart's letters, rambling on about his lunches and dinners in huge detail, to Rossini's drastic career change, music and food go together hand in hand it seems.

Our wonderful friends from the Düsseldorf orchestra certainly had that element down to perfection. The twinning projects with them were always a joy. Their conductor in those early years, Eberhard, was a great musician, who loved sharing experiences of music and conducting, as well as stories of love and passion. And he had a lot of them, especially the stories of love and passion. In those luxurious surroundings of the dressing room at the Düsseldorf Tonhalle, he would take me into his confidence, describing a colourful amorous life that often made me walk onto the stage blushing. I really adored him, he was a true musical friend and ally, and the way he could shape a Strauss waltz into the real thing is still an inspiration. Those dotted rhythms, almost on the beat, slightly delayed, it was perfection every time. I call them the *Eberhard* now, and everybody immediately knows what is required. I loved the concerts with him, and when I wasn't conducting, I would happily play piano parts or anything that needed filling in. Their new conductor was very talented, and not shy of lengthy rehearsals (as I found out at that final concert, trying to tame the little keyboard), but it just added to the fun of it all.

Eating and drinking beer together seemed equally as important as the music, and it was something everyone indulged in, to the max. *Brauerei Schumacher* was the favourite place to go to, just set back from the historic centre of the city. Home-brewed beer would flow throughout the night and the most amazing and indulgent dishes would appear from the kitchen, whilst we talked and laughed, and ate and drank. Celebrating life and friendship, and our music making got better with it, I swear.

Their pork knuckle was iconic, but the mushroom goulash was fabulous too. So fabulous in fact that it would be wrong not to follow in the footsteps of Mozart and Rossini and share a recipe of it. The one by Julia, from the *Zucker und Jagdwurst* vegan food blog. This is like a Brahms symphony, and the symbol of coming together through music. It makes life better, it really does.

For the potato dumplings
800g waxy potatoes, unpeeled
100g potato starch
50g flour
50g softened butter (vegan, if preferred)
2 slices white bread
Salt and pepper
Nutmeg

For the goulash

50g dried porcini, soaked in hot water for at least 30 minutes

700ml hot water

4 carrots

250g fresh mushrooms

10g fresh thyme

250ml red wine (vegan, if preferred)

2 onions

2 garlic cloves

6 tbsp tomato paste

3 tbsp mustard

2 tbsp soy sauce

300ml vegetable broth

Vegetable oil for frying

Salt and pepper

For the red cabbage

1 onion

1 apple

1 jar pre-cooked red cabbage

Vegetable oil for frying

Salt and pepper

Method

Step 1

Clean and chop the fresh mushrooms and carrots. Peal and finely dice the onions and garlic. Pluck the thyme leaves from their stems and finely chop. Once the dried porcini have softened, drain them, reserving the broth. Then chop the porcini.

Step 2

Cut the white bread into small pieces. Heat the (vegan) butter or vegetable oil in a frying pan and fry the bread until crispy and golden brown. If you prefer to use an oven for this, transfer the diced bread to a baking sheet, drizzle with olive oil, and bake at 180°C/355°F until golden brown. (If you want to save time at this point, use a toaster to crisp the bread, cutting it into smaller pieces afterwards).

Step 3

Add the unpeeled potatoes to a pan, cover with cold water and season with salt. Bring to a boil, then simmer over a medium heat for approx. 20 minutes, or until the potatoes are done. Drain and let them steam to cool down a bit.

Step 4

Whilst the potatoes are boiling, heat oil in a frying pan over a medium-low heat. Add onions and fry until translucent. Add the chopped carrots, fresh and soaked mushrooms, garlic and thyme. Stir to combine and fry for approx. 10 minutes. Then add tomato paste, mustard and soy sauce and keep frying for approx. 3 minutes. Deglaze with red wine and let simmer for a further 5 minutes. Now add the mushroom broth and vegetable broth and season generously with salt and pepper. Let the ragout simmer until you have made the potato dumplings, and season to taste just before serving.

Step 5

The boiled potatoes should be cooled by now. Peel and mash them until the texture is really smooth. There shouldn't be any lumps. Add potato starch, flour and softened (vegan) butter. Season with salt and pepper and knead the mixture into a smooth dough.

Step 6

Divide the dough into 8 same-sized pieces. One by one, take a portion of dough into one hand and press it into a disk. Add some of the crispy bread pieces into the middle, then fold the dough around it to form a nice round ball. Here's your potato dumpling! Repeat with the remaining dough.

Step 7

Bring a pan of salted water to a simmer (it shouldn't boil). Add the potato dumplings and let them simmer for approx. 20 minutes. After 20 minutes, remove one of the potato dumplings from the pan, cut off a smaller piece, and try it to see if it's done.

Step 8

Whilst the potato dumplings are boiling, prepare the red cabbage. We're using jarred red cabbage to save time, but you could also prepare cooked red cabbage from scratch. Peel and finely chop the onion. Cut the apple into smaller cubes. Heat vegetable oil in a pan and fry the onion and apple for approx. 3 minutes, or until the onion is translucent. Add jarred red cabbage and season with salt and pepper (you could also add a bay leaf or cloves). Add a splash of water to the pan, cover with a lid and let the red cabbage simmer over a medium-low heat until the potato dumplings are done.

Step 9

Remove the potato dumplings from the pan, allow to drain, then serve with the mushroom ragout and red cabbage.

This feast is best enjoyed with a dark beer or red wine and amazing people... Just in case you can't make it to *Schumacher's* in time for that life affirming post-concert supper.

> *'Eating, loving, singing and digesting are, in truth, the four acts of the comic opera, known as life. And they pass like bubbles of a bottle of champagne. Whoever lets them break without having enjoyed them is a complete fool.'*
> *Gioachino Rossini*

The mystery of sound

> *'Perhaps the chief requirement of the conductor is that they be humble before the composer; that they never interpose themselves between the music and the audience and that all their efforts, however strenuous or glamorous, are made in the service of the composer's meaning. The music itself is the whole reason for the conductor's existence.'*
> *Leonard Bernstein*

People often ask what exactly a conductor does. And after all these years, it is still an incredibly difficult question to answer.

They bring order, hopefully, by providing a beat with a pulse that everyone can turn to. In bigger orchestras, not every section can hear what is going on and so that central 'beat point' is certainly important. But as I found out again and again, orchestras will manage without it as well. And there is of course much more to a performance than playing in the same speed, whilst keeping an eye out for the dynamic markings. The choice of tempo itself and the extent of the tempo changes, how far to take the dynamic peaks, these are all just the start of an interpretation.

Mahler famously told a student that 'Allegro' means something different every time you play a piece. Allegro means 'happy' after all and doesn't come wrapped up with a specific metronome marking on the label. Sergei Rachmaninoff made different recordings of many of his own works, and it is interesting to hear how many liberties he took with the tempi from one version to the next.

So there again, a conductor has an important task and some big decisions to make. And the best conductors do so based on musical convictions, grown from knowledge, mixed with their own reflections and emotional input. But crucially, also affected by what the orchestra brings to the table with their playing. I have hardly ever heard an orchestra complain about the specific musical choices of a conductor. But I have heard them complain a lot about the lack of these, or a refusal to be 'with' the orchestra when these decisions are unfolding 'in play'.

Then there is the emotion itself, which comes to life through the conductor's communication and the players' reaction to it. The difference between Leonard Bernstein and, say, Pierre Boulez, could not be greater.

Boulez would conduct with clarity and an understanding of phrasing, balance and musical detail, but almost resisting bringing emotion into it. As the music has a lot within itself and the players will inevitably let some of their own feelings 'escape', the results can be fascinating, as his Wagner *Ring Cycles* proved.

Bernstein would make love to the orchestra and the audience at the same time. His genuine emotion would have the composer's soul as its direct source, and he would channel this for the whole world to see and feel. What set him apart though, is that he also displayed total control of the musical structure, and he would combine these like no one else could. When Bernstein cried, it was because the composer had done so when giving the world their heart in sound.

But to just stand there crying and flapping your arms around in an emotional way will only stifle the orchestra's ability to ride that wave. As Bernstein himself said, 'technique is communication', and he was right. It takes years of training and experience to be able to guide an orchestra to their best playing. 'Clarity brings freedom', Haitink told me all the time, and it is of course the same thing. Freedom for the players, but also freedom for the conductor, enabling them to be 'with' the orchestra all the way. And for the greatest and most successful conductors, this skill is something that they continue to hone until the last day they stand in front of an orchestra.

Of the many impressive concerts I was lucky enough to hear and see, two immediately rise to the top, and both happen to be the Vienna Philharmonic Orchestra performing Bruckner with Bernard Haitink conducting. These are Bruckner's Ninth Symphony at the *Salzburger Festspiele* in 2013 (with gratitude to my very generous family for financially enabling this!), and his Seventh Symphony during Haitink's farewell concerts seven years later. And what still comes back to me now is the sound of those performances. Never had I, nor have I since, heard such a sound within which everything unfolded.

Haitink took reasonably broad speeds. Not slow by any means but giving space for phrases to breathe. However, these were performances of high drama, drive and emotion, all of which came through in the sound.

How is it that a sound can be at the same time warm and golden but also thin and eerie, as it should be in many moments of the Ninth? How can a sound be feverishly hysterical, but also noble? And how is it possible that this sound comes from one person at the helm? The orchestra were able to give back that sound, and the whole emotional world it created, but it clearly came from the source that was Haitink. In 2013 he still did so with vigorous physical instructions whereas at those last concerts he had become more gestural, being frailer in his older age. But his technique was so strong, with that unsurpassed upbeat still powerfully present, that nothing seemed diminished at all, even at the very end of his career.

Haitink himself would say he had learned that doing less is more, and this is often true. But for me it seemed that he was just being more economical, like Karajan had done. He was 90 at this point! The flame of inspiration was still present and there was no doubt whatsoever that he was still firmly in control, again, just like Karajan had been. Both of them completely understood how an orchestra 'moves' and allowed for that movement to become part of their own musical vision. Almost like curling or manoeuvring a massive iceberg through a vast ocean.

Watching Bernstein, in contrast, we see a very different approach. He conducts in a much more controlling way, subdividing almost every turn and moment where he wants a bit of space or a subtle tempo change. Bernstein, maybe more than anyone else, was able to make an orchestra function like a single instrument, or a voice. There was never any compromise with the freedom he would take, just as he would when playing the piano. And through that, he was able to make Schumann's symphonies sound like his songs and let Mahler's symphonies unfold with a clarity and emotional transparency that, in my opinion, no one can touch.

Bernstein in his prime would allow for a certain freedom from the score's instructions, to be able to present us with the clearest vision of the composer, even if that sounds like a contradiction. He knew exactly how we as the audience would experience the music in a performance. His sound was totally unique to him, as was Karajan's sound to Karajan, Haitink's to Haitink, and Mariss Janssons' to Janssons.

The mystery of sound.

Many articles are written about it, and many people have tried to put a scientific explanation on it. The movement from the players, the instruments they play, or the acoustics of the concert venue. But all fall short. An orchestra will sound different in the same venue but with another conductor in front of them. Even the greatest of orchestras.

Hearing the difference in the sound of the Concertgebouw Orchestra under Bernard Haitink and then Ricardo Chailly was huge. Chailly is an awesome conductor, with a very 'inviting' beat, but somehow the sound seemed to have lost some of that freedom and silvery warmth. It was by no means worse, but it was different. And then Mariss Janssons brought back that earlier sound, perhaps with an even more seductive flow and shine to it.

Of course, as far as the string sections go, choices of bowings will make a difference. An extra bow will bring a 'renewal', and it is fair to say that the 'big sound' orchestras are less shy of a few extra bows than others. But it isn't just that.

One of the most eye-opening (or should I say ear-opening) experiences for me was whilst sitting in on a conducting workshop at the Vienna Hochschule, where my friend was studying at the time. Five different conducting students climbed onto the rostrum and played through Mendelssohn's *A Midsummer Night's Dream* overture. And before any instruction was given, and with exactly the same bowings, the college orchestra sounded different every single time. It all just happened with each conductor's arrival. Some of their movements were clearly asking for a specific sound, but even without those (and there were plenty examples of it that morning), there was an obvious change.

The mystery of sound.

Many years ago, the orchestral sound was something that was much more acknowledged and cultivated. There was the famous 'American sound', of which the Philadelphia Orchestra was perhaps the most prominent exponent. Rich, but clear, and full of melancholy. Nourished into greatness by people like Eugene Ormandy and Leopold Stokowski.

Stokowski introduced unsynchronized bowing, which freed up the sound, and he started conducting without a baton to encourage more flow in the playing. Both he and Ormandy didn't shy away from tweaking the orchestration at times, with Ormandy shamelessly doubling string sections when possible. Sergei Rachmaninoff was totally captivated by the orchestra's sound, calling it 'more Russian than Viennese', and he dedicated his Third Symphony to them. Their recording of it, with Rachmaninoff conducting, sends emotional shivers through our system. There is no sentimentality anywhere, everything comes purely from the sound.

Karajan's Berlin Philharmonic sound seemed to be ever renewing, and had this burnished quality, but was also incredibly dynamic. Van Beinum's and Haitink's Concertgebouw Orchestra sound was more mellow, with a deep silvery glow. And the miracle that still is the Vienna Philharmonic sound, with total clarity, like a chamber orchestra, yet also an intensity and depth few can touch.

It is sadly true that these specific qualities seem to be fading away, and most orchestras will sound much more alike these days. The finger is being pointed at the perfection of the digital recording process, or a specific 'need' in the commercial world of selling these recordings and concerts. But perhaps it is also because nowadays, principal conductors spend so much less time with 'their' orchestra and appear to be at the helm of at least three of them at the same time. And maybe that art of honing, and dare I say 'owning' a sound is just dying out with the world moving further and further away from it.

Even more remarkable to me is the difference in the sound of pianists. This is such a 'high tech' instrument, with so many mechanical steps taking place between a finger touching a key and the sound we hear coming out. Yet every player will bring their own specific sound to that same instrument. A rich and almost orchestral sound, a clearer pianistic sound, or, if we are unlucky, a biting harsh sound.

And then there is someone like Artur Rubinstein who keeps the whole world in his sound. We suddenly stop talking of the above parameters, but move to a deep emotion, melancholy, desperation. And all this in the sound alone. Rubinstein would famously put any musical 'effect', like use of excessive rubato and tempo changes, through what Daniel Barenboim called his 'filter of necessity'. Rubinstein's playing was in the uppermost league of tasteful and effect free. Yet he would move us totally, primarily by the sound, and the emotion he would infuse through his hands, as a direct connection to his soul. Lucky us, who were brought up on his playing.

There is a touching moment in the film of him performing Brahms' First Piano Concerto, with a very young Haitink conducting the Concertgebouw Orchestra. In the first chorale-like solo episode, Haitink turns to Rubinstein and looks at him with clear adoration, but also with an intention to take it all in, as if to be able to share it again and again. No tricks, just a noble and almost simple unfolding of the music, made epic through the depth of his sound. I saw that look again during the Bruckner 9 in Salzburg, when the Vienna strings were creating pure gold. Haitink stopped waving his arms, and just looked at the section with that same admiration and gratitude. It moved us to tears, as it also did the orchestra and Haitink himself.

The greatest compliment I can be given is that the orchestra I conducted had 'sounded good'. And I am narcissistically proud that it seems to be something that I am able to draw out of an orchestra. I realise that being clear is a crucial element of that.

After conducting the wonderful (and not nearly enough performed) Grace Williams Violin Concerto in Bristol, with the star soloist Stephen Bryant, I was so happy that the players thanked me for always making sure that everyone knew where they were. But this is the result from all those years of learning from harsh task masters, conducting amateur opera and being able to work with incredible people in fantastic orchestras. And I never stop aiming to improve that tool of communication, technique. With it, 'making sound' is enabled somehow. But how exactly is still not a science, and never will be. It often just starts to happen by playing and then playing again.

I have been so lucky to have worked with singer Hans, who could set off emotion in his voice without ever being over the top. And I have been lucky to have had Alan Weiss, passionately sharing with us the world of the great musicians of our time. And my Russian teacher, who put into words exactly what 'sound' should contain. I guess I have also been lucky that Artur Rubinstein's piano playing filled my parental home for many hours on end (with apologies to my older brother, who was less keen on his Brahms than I was). And most of all, I was lucky to have been able to sit behind Bernard Haitink and see and hear that sound starting to flow from him, through his baton. In the Opera House, but also at his own kitchen table, without any orchestra even present. I guess I absorbed all these things and found my way of sharing it.

What does a conductor do?

A conductor can make the orchestra fly and play their best. Bring everything and everyone together and make it 'one'. And when that happens, the orchestral sound is the most intoxicating and addictive substance to float on. Just as it had totally overwhelmed me as a child in the slow movement of Bruch's First Violin Concerto, and still does now. And at that very moment I realise I am the luckiest person alive. Being part of it and being at the centre of creating it with wonderful musicians.

Life is moving on, and new opportunities and positive challenges await. These last near thirty years on the island that is Great Britain shaped me into the musician I am now. Arriving there as a young student and from then on having been on this colourful, at times insane, but always inspiring journey.

It has been a total privilege to be part of so many musical families, with all their ups and downs, like all families. But I am most proud of all the music we have created, making life itself better, as only music can do. I might have left the island, but I am not ready to leave conducting, let alone music.

Not yet please. Not yet for a long, long time.

Acknowledgments

'Writing it all down' was a direct result of long and colourful conversations with friends and colleagues, often accompanied by many glasses of red wine. Since our move to Spain, these conversations turned more and more towards the musical adventures of the last 28 years, but also what all these experiences meant for my own music making. And through that, the question of what it takes to be a conductor. Without all the wonderful people that have been, and still are, part of my musical life, none of it would have been possible.

I am forever grateful to my mother, who lovingly provided a world where classical music was a beautiful thing of enjoyment and enrichment, without it ever being something that was pushed. Grateful for her asking me half an hour before my piano lessons if I might do some practice for maybe ten minutes, just so that my teacher wouldn't have to go through the same scenario again as the previous Wednesday. 'Do it for them?' Grateful for a home full of wonderful support, but never insistence.

Apart maybe from her sitting my brother and I down every Easter to experience at least two *St. Matthew Passions*, complete with live running commentary, recit by recit, aria by aria, and vocalist by vocalist. She was a *Matthew Passion* fanatic (freaking out many an Evangelist or Judas by sitting on the front row, mouthing every single word from memory), and she had standards, which were rarely met. But when they passed muster, Hallelujah! (apologies for the wrong quote and composer). My brother doesn't share the classical music bug, but these times forged a bond that is unbreakable. Apologies to my mother from the both of us for not making her two life wishes come true, singing in a *Passion* as a boy soprano, or taking up the double bass! And a huge thank you to my brother for putting up with all the Bach, Mozart, Brahms and Chopin during those years.

My wonderful Oma Nettie, who had made music and going to concerts such a positive part of her children's lives, and also ours, her grandchildren. And making it fun. Too much so on one occasion. She should never have pointed out the strapless top starting to slide down from the pianist's back, followed by frantic attempts to rescue the situation whilst playing a Beethoven concerto. Hysterical laughter was hard to suppress, and only partly achieved.

My incredible teachers. All of them, but mostly Didi and Alan, who stirred the passion and made a life of making music an absolute necessity.

And thank you to best friend Esther, whose professional and human skills got me through some exciting times when confronted with a big emotional culture divide.

To incredible Sally, for spending ages trying to turn my rambling musings into decent English!

And to my better half Nick, for being there always, and for getting it. And for providing the illustrations, without ever losing patience with me!

When writing this book, I turned to many publications and articles for support, providing me with detailed information about musicians, locations and much more. A few stand out:

– Michael Steen's *The Lives and Times of Great Composers* is one of the most eye-opening pieces of writing, and a life companion of mine for many years.

– *Conversations with Karajan* by Richard Osborne, shows the great conductor as the true human being he was, with a sense of wisdom, purpose and humour too.

– The enlightening article from the 2013 *Italy Magazine* on Verdi and his *Un ballo in maschera* and the ever inspiring and delightful letters by Mozart and Chopin.

We are lucky that we live in an era where recordings are a luxury we can take for granted, and they feature generously in this story. Many of these I first experienced in their original LP or video form, before CDs and DVDs/Blu-ray took over. Now, most recordings will be available to stream from various sources. Where known, I have added the company which released the CD or DVD version.

– *Rubinstein in Concert*. Beethoven/Brahms Piano concertos, plus solo selection. Artur Rubinstein, Concertgebouw Orchestra, Bernard Haitink. DVD, Deutsche Grammophon

– *Mahler, The Symphonies, Das Lied von der Erde*. Leonard Bernstein, London Symphony Orchestra, Israel Philharmonic Orchestra, Vienna Philharmonic Orchestra. DVD, Deutsche Grammophon

— *Mahler, Symphony No.9.* Herbert Von Karajan, Berliner Philharmoniker. 1982 live. CD, Deutsche Grammophon

— *Mahler, Symphony No.9.* Bruno Walter, Vienna Philharmonic Orchestra, 1938. CD EMI

— *Schumann, The Symphonies.* Leonard Bernstein, Vienna Philharmonic Orchestra. DVD Deutsche Grammophon

— *Rimsky-Korsakov, Scheherazade.* Leopold Stokowski, London Symphony Orchestra, 1974. CD, Decca

— *Debussy, Prélude à l'après midi d'un faune/Nocturnes/Iberia.* Leopold Stokowski, London Symphony Orchestra. CD, EMI

— *Debussy, Prélude à l'après midi d'un faune/Nocturnes/Pelleas et Melisande Suite.* Claudio Abbado, Berliner Philharmoniker. CD, Deutsche Grammophon

— *Wagner, Der Ring des Nibelungen, excerpts.* Deborah Polaski. Daniel Barenboim, Chicago Symphony Orchestra. CD, Elatus

— *Rachmaninoff, Complete piano concertos.* Sergei Rachmaninoff, Philadelphia Orchestra, Leopold Stokowski, Eugene Ormandy. CD, RCA

— *Rachmaninoff, Symphony No.3, Vocalise, The Isle of the Dead.* Sergei Rachmaninoff, Philadelphia Orchestra. CD, Naxos/RCA

— *Bruckner, Symphony No.9,* Bernard Haitink, Orchestre National de France. Live 2015. France Music Concerts, live stream

— *Bruckner, Symphony No.9,* Herbert von Karajan, Vienna Philharmonic. Live 1978, DVD, Deutsche Grammophon

— *Bruckner, Symphony No.9,* Leonard Bernstein, Vienna Philharmonic. DVD, Deutsche Grammophon

— *Berliner Philharmoniker, Europakonzert 1993.* Bernard Haitink, Berliner Philharmoniker. DVD, EuroArts

– *Debussy, La Mer*. Claudio Abbado, Luzern Festival Orchestra. DVD/stream, EuroArts

– *Mozart, Symphonies No.40 and 41*. Bruno Walter, Columbia Symphony Orchestra. CD, CBS

– *Liszt, Sonata /Franck/Bach-Busoni*. Artur Rubinstein. CD RCA

– *Rachmaninoff, Rhapsody on a Theme by Paganini/Piano Concerto No.2*. Artur Rubinstein, Chicago Symphony Orchestra, Fritz Reiner. CD, RCA

– *Dvorak, Symphony No.7*. Jiri Belohlavek, Czech Philharmonic Orchestra. DVD, Decca

– *Wagenaar, Cyrano de Bergerac/Overtures*. Riccardo Chailly, Royal Concertgebouw Orchestra. CD Decca

– *Diepenbrock, Im Grossen Schweigen*. Hakan Hagegard, Riccardo Chailly, Royal Concertgebouw Orchestra. CD, Decca

About the author

Stephan Dorré was born in Haarlem, the Netherlands, in 1972. Surrounded by music from an early age, it was the flute that enticed him initially, before moving on to the piano and conducting.

Stephan left school early to study at the Utrecht Conservatoire, obtaining his solo piano diploma in 1995. He then moved to London to make orchestral conducting his main professional focus.

Stephan has been Musical Director and guest conductor for several orchestras and opera companies in the UK and he conducts professional engagements throughout Europe. He is also very busy as a pianist, focussing on chamber music and *Lieder* accompaniment, and working with some of the Netherlands' foremost vocalists.

Writing has always been a great passion for Stephan (after it became clear that his hopes of becoming a professional tennis player weren't realistic), and came to the fore during the Covid lockdown years, first by writing informal blogs, followed by columns and longer articles. *Let's try that again* is Stephan's first full-length book.

Alora, July 2024

Mariposa Press 24-2